Author J. Timothy King opens his heart, sharing the passions, pains, and triumphs of the life-hazing we all must undergo in the search for romance and true love.

In this unforgettable book, Tim reveals the embarrassing and sometimes juicy secrets from his own past, which led him ultimately to true love.

Heartbreaking and heartwarming, this true love story is sure to inspire and encourage all who seek true love, or have already found it.

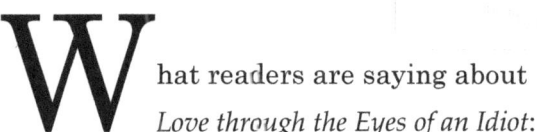

W hat readers are saying about *Love through the Eyes of an Idiot*:

You're such a romantic! You're very honest and frank in your approach. It's refreshing.
    -Doug O.

Upon reading "You Never Forget Your First Crush," p. 13:
You've captured something so completely universal. The angst of unrequited love. I found myself blushing in commiseration.
    -Kim

Referring to "Affections," p. 100:
Even love unreturned can be beautiful, like your poem.
    -Melissa K.

You are about to relive with me my own heartrending search for love and happiness. This quest took me to the very edge of despair, before lifting me to the heights of joy.

Along the way, you'll:
- feel the passion and affection, the turmoil of rejection and the peace of acceptance;
- laugh along, looking back at my youthful foibles;
- ride shotgun through my love-life, as I go too fast, and as I go too slow;
- discover why some people (like I did) always fall in love with the wrong people, and how to break the pattern;
- see inside the mind of a true, hard-core romantic;
- find hope that there might actually be somebody for everybody, someone to heal the loneliness;
- meet Delilah, the radio DJ, who became the big sister I needed, when I needed her, reached into my devastated life, and turned it around;
- hear my own father, in the finest tradition, advise me on how to make a marriage work;
- discover why relationships do not have to decay with age, and how a relationship can get better and more passionate the longer it goes on.

The journey will require character and persistence, because it's an intense and arduous one, until we ultimately discover the secret of love.

Turn the page, and let's begin...

through the Eyes of an Idiot

A True Story of Finding the Secret of Love, Sex, and Romance

J. Timothy King

The names and personal details of some characters in the following account have been changed.

Cover art: The author's eyes, as drawn by his daughter Abbie, age 10.

Love through the Eyes of an Idiot
A True Story of Finding the Secret of Love, Sex, and Romance

Copyright © 2009 J. Timothy King. All rights reserved.

Published by J. Timothy King.
http://www.JTimothyKing.com/

First trade paperback edition, July 2009.
Printed in the United States of America.

ISBN 978-0-9816925-2-4

10   9   8   7   6   5   4   3   2   1

Table of Contents

Preface.. 1
Forward... 4
1. The Ones that Got Away................................... 7
2. You Never Forget Your First Crush................. 13
3. The Blonde in the Pink Sweater...................... 20
4. The Sister I Never Had..................................... 29
5. The Crushes Between....................................... 36
6. On Again, Off Again.. 41
7. A Search for Meaning....................................... 48
8. The Heartbreak Girl.. 53
9. Only Just Friends.. 60
10. Ain't Nothin' But a Horn Dog........................ 66
11. A Transforming Thought................................ 76
12. Happily Ever After.. 87
Romantic Poems.. 96
   Lifelong Romance.. 97
   To the One I Love.. 98
   Thinking of You.. 99
   Affections.. 100
   If Only I Could Have Your Love..................... 101
   Blue and Grey... 102
   Dear Tracy... 104
   Margaret.. 106
Pine... 108

The following story is true, but the names of all characters have been changed, with the following exceptions: Delilah Rene (a.k.a. Dee) and her friend Re, and my wife Margaret.

To my wife Margaret, my best friend and the love of my life, with whom I find myself falling more deeply in love on every new day.

Preface

When I say "idiot," it's a joke, a little bit. But also serious.

It may sound like I'm being harsh on myself. After all, what I went through is just par for the course. I was not a bad kid, or a backwards kid, or a troubled kid. My experiences were typical of what a teenager then young adult experiences. The details of my experience were only mine, of course, but we all go through the same feelings, the same challenges, the same idiocy.

But I truly believe I was "an idiot"—not stupid, just idiotic, at least when it came to love. And it was making me miserable.

But idiocy is one of the realities of life. The difference between idiocy and genius is simply whether or not what you try works. In the beginning, when one tries something new, he fails, because it's the first time he's tried, and he doesn't know what he's doing. He fails over and over again, until he finally figures out the secret, and then he succeeds. Then he's a genius.

We're all born idiots, but then we learn. Being an

idiot is part of learning, part of life.

I, too, eventually learned how to be happy in love.

It may also sound like I as a teenager or young adult was hard on myself. Maybe I was. But that again is part of the idiocy, the baptism of fire we all have to go through in order to grow up.

You see, idiocy is also why the young learn so much more and accomplish so much more than many adults. As it turns out, "idiot" should be a term of endearment, because being an idiot is a good thing: it means you're stretching yourself beyond what you already know, putting yourself in emotional danger, experiencing failure and hurt and despair, learning what you can from it, and then trying again.

Going through my old papers, in preparation for writing this book, I ran across an old something my father had written in 1991. And it struck me as uniquely apropos to this narrative:

> We must remember that history cannot be written properly until it is recalled in the light of tomorrow's achievements and the fulfillment of tomorrow's promises...
>
> When we stand before Him Who has been watching our steps when we did not know where they would fall, Who has been holding our hand when we could not see the way, Whose voice we heard often when

the silence of loneliness would otherwise overwhelm us, then we will know. Then we will see clearly how God's grace first charted our course and then the providence of God led us down it.

There's a lesson here. We tend to dismiss the idiots, especially in love. We tend to be very picky, and even to look down on those who seem less than us. But if we are wise, we will remember that there is none so inexperienced as to be beyond hope, as long as he is sincere.

God bless all the idiots! May all their heartbreak turn to gold.

Forward

My family, my friends, those who know me best, may be surprised at what I reveal in these stories—shocked even. In these pages, you will learn things about me that you never knew and maybe never even suspected. You may have had no idea exactly what I was going through, because I was a quiet, private kid. I usually didn't share my feelings, spending most of my time wrapped up in my own thoughts, preferring to solve problems myself (or dwell on them) rather than to ask for help of those who had already solved them.

I have tried to portray my experiences with as much veracity as possible, drawing on old journals, letters, and notes, as well as my own memory. But please remember that this record is really only my *perception* regarding these experiences. The characters in the story are really only my *perceptions* of the real people behind them. In other words, you're getting only my side of the story.

This is why I've used pseudonyms throughout, with only a few specific exceptions. Because not only did these events take place many years ago, and people change, but also is this story my own subjective, limited, one-sided view of complex events, involving complex people. Therefore, even though no one looks bad in the story (except maybe me), I still try to protect the true identity of the characters in the story.

Exceptions to this rule include my wife Margaret, and my parents (whom I don't actually mention by name). But the one big exception to the rule is Delilah, the nationally syndicated radio DJ, who like a big sister became a close friend and advisor to me just when I needed her most. I use her real name, because she already has more publicity than I could ever give or take away from her, and on that pulpit, she can adequately correct any errors I inadvertently make in her story. Not so with the other characters in the book.

This book is part history and part confession. Writing it has ironically allowed me to reconnect with many of the people in this story, people with whom I had lost contact, people for whom I cared deeply, people like Dylan and Dave, Mandy and Enola, and especially Lita Ortiz.

In the Bible, Christ's mission was to create "a new covenant" with God, as we say. But that's actually a bit of a misstatement. A better way to say it would be that He *renewed* our relationship with God, because he executed a fresh agreement, of grace rather than of justice.

In the same way, it overjoys me that writing this book has allowed me to reconnect with old friends. I hope that it clarifies to them what I was going through and all the good they did for me, sometimes just by being there. And I pray that these renewed friendships will now grow in the light of all that we've learned since then.

Many of the following confessions are hard for me to make, because they are still full of emotion. Digging up these old memories, reading through my old journals, letters, and other papers, preparing this manuscript, all have fired up old feelings, some affectionate, some loving, some hurtful, all passionate. At one point, I thought my word processor had corrupted 2 days worth of work, and I felt devastated, because I simply did not want to relive those 2 days. My wife Margaret has been most supportive throughout this process, once even allowing me to cuddle up with her and cry on her breast, because I had just finished writing a particularly gut-wrenching scene. I love her more than anyone could ever know.

1. The Ones that Got Away

I remember the first time I made a woman blush. I don't remember her name. Actually, she was little more than a girl, and I was still a boy, a child, an idiot in fact. I would remain an idiot until just before I got engaged.

We were in our early twenties, and we still thought of ourselves as kids, not adults. She was a temp, filling in as receptionist at the office where I worked. And she was cute, real cute. Her dirty blonde hair revealed the soft features of neck and jaw. I lost track of how much time I blew chatting with her rather than doing work. (I didn't get fired.)

She said she had a boyfriend, and I believed her. I've never liked lies, even little white lies, intended to manipulate people. So if the boyfriend story was a fib, I didn't want to know it.

She also said the relationship with her boyfriend wasn't serious. I caught the hint; by that time, I was no longer ignorant. But I was uncomfortable getting involved with someone who would break up with her so-called boyfriend for me. How much a boyfriend could he be if she'd ditch him the second another guy comes along? Did I want to be in that situation? At least these were the thoughts running through my head, whether or not they were justified. I was looking for a relationship, and if she'd break up with him to go with me, what would stop her from breaking up with me on account of someone else? I wasn't stupid; just idiotic.

On the last day of her job with us, I knew I would miss wasting time with her. This was it, she said; she wouldn't be back.

"That's a shame," I said.

She looked at the carpet and smiled, and her face changed from freckled cream to some shade of pink.

Sometimes I think women don't realize the power they hold, how good it makes a man feel to please a woman.

I should've gotten her phone number. I should've given her mine. True, maybe we would never have used them. But I didn't even think of that. I simply wrote off the opportunity.

In retrospect, I believe the reason was that she was too available.

I had no real excuse. It wasn't like it had been with the girl who sat next to me in my high-school French class. She was friendly and perky, and prettier than most. One day we were studying the use of the verb

1. The Ones that Got Away

aimer. The teacher gave a quick rundown of phrases, after which the girl turned to me and lightheartedly remarked, apropos of nothing, *"Je t'aime beaucoup!"* This means "I like you a lot!" and it's something that a girl might say to a boy she wouldn't mind dating.

I heard her. I understood. I said nothing. I didn't think of myself as handsome or cute, or a ladies' man. I didn't know how to flirt with girls. I didn't know what to say. So I didn't even smile. I was such an idiot.

Yes, I have a way with the ladies. But at least back then I had the excuse of being a quiet, awkward teenager who didn't know how to put one and one together to make two.

Not so, years later, when I met the flight attendant. I knew that's what she did for a living, because she told me. I knew she had an interesting, steady job. I knew her mother. And the girl was nice. She actually talked to me and listened to me and seemed interested in learning who I was. And I had fun learning about who she was. And she was pretty, too pretty. These were all problems, of course.

I could've fallen in love with her. Hell, she took my breath away. I remember the pool party at which I had to divert my eyes to keep from staring. And even then, my mind continued to stare. When she smiled, dimples appeared in her cheeks, and her eyes lit up the room like candles. Her blonde curls and beautiful figure might make a man think she might have been an actress or a model.

Even so, she still made me comfortable enough to carry on a conversation. And we had some fun, casual talks. She always approached me, though; I never would have approached her.

From me, not even a nibble.

I don't know if she would have been interested in a relationship, but I didn't even bother to consider it. Why not? In retrospect, I believe it was because she appeared basically normal, and therefore available. So I didn't long to be with her. There was no magic.

In another instance, some old friends of my parents had visited from out of state, along with their son and teenage daughter. I was pushing 16 at the time, and she was only 12½. She was cute and sweet, a nice girl, as far as I could tell. After they had left on their trek back home, I found a small, folded note in my room. On the front were the words "To Tim." I unfolded the paper and read, "I like you very much," and she signed her name.

I did nothing, said nothing, as if I had never even found the note, the same as I had to the girl in French class.

During the following year, she mailed me several more times, and I opened and read her letters, but I failed to answer even one.

1. The Ones that Got Away

I think I just didn't want to deal with it, because of our age difference, although that may not have been fair to her. After all, the previous year, I had torn my heart apart for Lita Ortiz, who was several months *even younger*. Or maybe it was that experience that kept me clammed up. But most likely it was simply that she presented no barrier, nothing to long for.

I don't know if anything ever would have come of it, after we both grew a little, because we lived so distant from each other. Still, I should have at least made contact with her.

Since then, we have indeed made contact, because her family and mine are still acquainted, even after all these years. I'm happy with how life turned out, as I hope she is, but I regretted that she didn't know that my lack of response was not because there was anything wrong with her, because there wasn't. In fact, that was the problem. As the cliché goes, it's not you; it's me. I simply felt nothing for her at the time, because she was too damn normal. Good for her, bad for me.

If ever I happened to be attracted to a normal, available girl, I would be sure to sabotage it. One girl I asked out on a date must have said yes too easily. On the phone, a couple days before our date, I gushed that I couldn't believe that *she* was actually going out with *me*.

She instantly changed her mind.

Oh well, easy come, easy go.

2. You Never Forget Your First Crush

I began getting interested in girls at the age of 12 and a half.

Before then, around the time I turned 12, there was one girl who was clearly interested in me, threw herself at me, which gave my father pause. At that time, he pastored a tiny church in the small town of Burgettstown, Pennsylvania, and he wisely advised me to be wary of such a girl. But it was just a little early for me to be interested in girls, and ironically, her parents didn't like me. So Dad really didn't have much to fear.

Nonetheless, she and I spoke on the phone a few times. Or rather, we held the receivers to our ears, me sprawled across our golden, plush, living-room carpet. We listened to each other breathe as the minutes ticked away on my wristwatch.

We also exchanged a letter or two, one of which I still have. She greeted me and the rest of the family, told me about the multiple-sclerosis read-a-thon (for which she had already collected over $100!), noted that her parents had separated, and expressed shock that the price of stamps had gone up to 20 cents a piece!

But I really didn't begin to become interested in girls until a pretty brunette with long, straight hair, pinned up on each side with a brown barrette, sat down at the piano in school chorus. I sat in the top row, all the way at the left, and I still remember her clearly. The director explained, Maryanne would accompany us as we sang certain numbers, but for now, she was just going to play a little something for us.

Maryanne proceeded to perform Gershwin's "Rhapsody in Blue," flawlessly, without the sheet music. The pretty blonde who sat next to me commented that Maryanne was really good. I agreed, not thinking that the pretty blonde was the one who would be giving me shoulder massages for the rest of the year, as part of our choral warm-ups. I was mesmerized by Maryanne as she played through complicated runs and chords.

Then, some minutes into the piece, she suddenly stopped and, embarrassed, apologized for not going on, because she forgot the rest. The choral director said that was quite all right, and we applauded. I probably applauded more loudly than anyone else in the room.

The first erotic dream I remember involved a girl in tight jeans. I didn't see her face, just her jeans. In my dream, I placed my hand in her back pocket, and it was fun, a lot of fun. But not just fun. It was emotional,

2. You Never Forget Your First Crush

passionate, romantic. The dream left a longing in my gut, a feeling that its memory still inspires today, not just sexual, but exciting, affectionate. I'm sure the dream was about Maryanne.

To this day, I have a penchant for long, dark hair and for names that begin with M and R.

As it turned out, Maryanne and I shared many of the same classes, and her last name was alphabetically just before mine, and many teachers assigned seating alphabetically. I spent the next two school years sitting behind her and falling in love with her beautiful hair. When she walked into class, I could smell her perfume, a light, winsome scent that stopped my breath and accelerated my heart. But I never told her how I felt.

Yes, I was an idiot, but you're allowed to be an idiot with your first crush. This is one of the cruel laws of nature.

I obsessed over this girl—creepy, yes, though harmless, at least harmless to her. In study hall, I sat several seats to her left and a couple rows behind, and I spent endless hours learning to sketch her profile, looking down, writing at her desk. She had olive skin and a short, concave nose and soft features, dark eyebrows, and brown eyes. Her hair flowed through her barrette, around the back of her ear, and over her shoulders. I could probably still draw her picture today, from memory.

One of the songs we learned in school chorus was "Endless Love," by Lionel Richie. I also learned to play it on the guitar, and I would sometimes sit outside on our porch swing, picking out music on my guitar, and thinking of her. To this day, every time I hear that song on the radio, I remember Maryanne.

I eventually wrote my own songs about her, some of the first songs I ever wrote and cheesy as any first-songs ever written. One of them, "Dream Girl," tells of the deep passion I felt. Another, untitled song says, "I see your face, and I dream of you every night, but why didn't you ever love me back?"

Looking back at that now, I want to scream at my young self, "Because you never gave her the chance, you idiot! You never told her how you feel. You never even said, 'Hello.' Never smiled at her. Never flirted with her. Nothing. There's nothing wrong with staring and smiling at a pretty girl, you know, if you want her to notice you."

But I had been afraid of rejection. I was a shy, socially inept kid. I didn't know how to flirt, and I didn't know how to look for signals of romantic interest. I also didn't know how to ask for help, even though I had around me those who could have taught me how to talk to girls. But I had deep, passionate feelings that I didn't want to talk about, for fear of being embarrassed, for fear of getting hurt, and just because

2. You Never Forget Your First Crush

I usually kept my feelings to myself.

At a school track event once, I sat in the bleachers behind Maryanne and her friends. The sun shone through a clear sky, warming everything it touched. The boy sitting next to her touched the top of her head. "Whoa!" he said to their other friends. "Hey, feel how hot Maryanne's hair is."

This was the same boy, as I recall, who later I saw petting her hair and smiling at her, and she was smiling back, and when I witnessed the exchange, a wave of jealousy and regret swept through my body. I didn't feel like going on with life anymore, and for a brief moment, I actually thought about death.

She was so out of my league: I was lonely and unpopular, while she was beautiful and surrounded herself with other beautiful people.

At the end of eighth grade, just after I had turned 14, my father got a new job. We were to move away from Burgettstown, to Sharpsville, about 100 miles north, and my last chance with Maryanne would be lost forever.

Sometime during the last few days of the school year, I let the cat out of the bag. I had told someone in the school that I liked her, and word had gotten around among her friends. The last day, in Science class, our classmates teased us about it. One of them found a strand of her hair and handed it to me. "And that's not even from her head!" he said.

At lunch, one of them invited me to sit next to her. My head was spinning. They told me to put my arm around her. I tried, wrapped my arm around her back, but I did it wrong and ended up touching her breast with my hand, to choruses of "Oooh!" One of them fixed my hand, placed it on her shoulder, as she simultaneously grinned and sunk in embarrassment. I knew they were aiming their mocking tones at me, and catching Maryanne in the crossfire, but I didn't care. I lived to regret that I had embarrassed her. But for a few moments, my consciousness completely filled with the simple feeling that I was sitting next to the prettiest girl in school.

Sometime after it was over, one of her friends had a little talk with me, a sober talk. She must have seen how depressed I was, because she said, "You really like her, don't you?" I nodded, but so strong were my feelings, they could only be described by one word: *love*. Not the kind of love with which you build a life together, but the kind of love that tears you apart from the inside and makes you lose your senses.

For about a month after my family moved, I cried myself to sleep, cuddling up with my pillow as though it were her, imagining impossible scenarios in which we might someday be reunited. It obviously never happened.

2. You Never Forget Your First Crush

Some years later, on a whim, I Googled her name, found one mention of her in all the Internet. After college, she had run in the state beauty pageant. She had come to within two awards of being Miss America.

I guess you're allowed to be an idiot for your first crush. But this unfortunate experience set up a pattern that would oft be repeated over the next decade.

3. The Blonde in the Pink Sweater

I was sitting in ninth-grade Geometry class one day in early Spring, 1984, minding my own business, when someone tossed onto my desk a sheet of paper, folded thrice. Any classwork we had that day was over, and we had been working independently, socializing, or just thinking. I unfolded the note and read:

> Tim,
>
> Hi. This is Erika. Will you dance with me at the dance? I love you. I'm the one in the pink sweater.
>
> Erika
>
> P.S. I like your notebook.

I knew it was a joke. I didn't like being teased, but I knew teasing when I saw it. "Dance"? "Love" me? Please! Some girl whom I didn't even know wanted to taunt the quiet nerd who got effortless A's in Geometry.

Still, my curiosity was piqued. I wanted at least to see who was making fun of me.

The previous year, my father had resigned his

3. The Blonde in the Pink Sweater

pastorate in Burgettstown in order to take a job at denominational headquarters, moving us to Sharpsville, PA. I had sat through almost a whole school year with the kids in this class, but I still didn't know who Erika was. I mostly kept to myself, had just a few friends, and didn't socialize with girls much.

I looked around and found the girl in the pink sweater, one seat over and one seat back. She filled out that sweater like Geena Davis, tall, curvy, with locks of yellow silk and cheeks like juicy apples. I was at the age at which a good issue of TV Guide had sufficient pulchritudinous value to serve as porn. So when I saw Erika, sexy as a TV star, I was... intrigued.

Her girlfriend was the one who had tossed me the note.

Somehow, they struck up a conversation with me. I'm sure I declined going to "the dance." We talked about various things, including premarital sex. I don't know what sparked the discussion. Maybe she just brought it up out of nowhere. As a pastor's kid, I had been raised to believe in chastity. I believed a person should wait for marriage, while she believed that it was worth trying out sexual partners.

As it turned out, she babysat for a family who lived in the same complex I did. Our townhouse was just a jaunt through the woods away from the high school, so I would walk to school in the morning, walk back in the afternoon. My parents had set up a bedroom for me in the finished basement, and when I wasn't programming my Commodore 64 in the living room, I could often be found playing my guitar downstairs or outside in the back yard.

One sunny spring Saturday, I walked or rode my bike—don't remember which—over to the unit where Erika babysat. Talking with her at the back door while the baby slept, she invited me up to the bedroom. I knew it was just a joke. Besides, her girlfriend was right there, standing next to us while we were talking. And even if I were the kind of guy who wanted to get down and dirty, getting amorous on her employer's bed still would have been too weird, not to mention risky—I didn't want her to lose her babysitting job. Even so, I wondered what it would be like to follow her up the stairs, sprawl out on the bed with her.

Then she asked if I wanted to kiss her.

Her girlfriend said in an encouraging tone, "I'll go in the other room."

"Yeah, she'll go into the other room," echoed Erika.

And the other girl slid, out of sight, into the kitchen.

"Kiss me," Erika ordered, as seductively as she could.

I knew she was probably gambling that I wouldn't actually go through with it. But I wanted to, and I would have if I could have. I stepped forward, on the

3. The Blonde in the Pink Sweater

verge of touching her, then froze, a heavy brick in my chest where my heart ought to have been, eyes wide, like a deer caught in the headlights.

I always wondered what would have happened if I had relaxed, if I had simply up and kissed her before she could object. Would she have kissed me back? What would it have felt like? How would she have smelled? How would she have tasted?

Most memories of that Spring have been lost to the ravages of time. I stayed in touch with Erika—easy since we went to the same school. By the end of May, I had developed quite a passion for her. The opposite of love is indifference, and the companion of love is rage. Words were spoken. Angers flared. At one point, drawing from the reaches of my vocabulary, I told her she was "an obnoxious, self-centered, egotistical, dirty, little, two-faced slime ball."

It just so happened, about that time, my father was to attend a weekend business meeting at a small college in Utica, NY, and the whole family came along for a weekend road trip. They put us up in a rustic dormitory, my parents in a suite with bathroom, refrigerator, stove, and even a kitchen sink. Meanwhile, my brother and I stayed in a smaller room two doors down the hall, and they brought up a crib for my youngest brother, who at that time was only a year old.

The sun that weekend scorched the air around us,

as well as anyone who braved the direct sunlight. And the spring pollen aggravated my allergies, leaving me with a runny nose and sore throat. My brother and I did our best to stay out of the open air, by using the "subway," a system of underground tunnels that connected the four buildings on campus. And we spent our time exploring, playing basketball, or even hide-and-seek.

Over the weekend, I grew sorry for lashing out at Erika as I had done, and I wrote a long letter not only apologizing but also telling her all about our trip to New York state.

The last day, as we were packing up to leave, I walked down the hallway of the dorm, and I happened to glance in one of the open doors to one of the other rooms. Inside, a pretty, young Latina with long, thick hair, was packing her things into a suitcase. I did not know her, but her youthful beauty stabbed into my innards. She looked up at me, and I stared for a moment, transfixed, before I quickly turned away and continued on, still reeling and amazed. That moment will forever be frozen in my memory.

We all piled into the car and drove about a half hour to someone's house—I didn't know whose at the time—where we would eat and sleep over until the following day, Sunday, because my father was to be a guest speaker in his church.

3. The Blonde in the Pink Sweater

Then I saw her again, the girl from the dormitory. She was there, at the same house.

As it turned out, the people we were staying with had a son, Dylan, about my age. And the girl, little Carmelita Ortiz, turned out to be younger than I had originally thought. Lita was three and a half years younger than I, and she had already been turning into a beautiful woman. Moreover, she was sweet and outgoing, and she made a boy feel he could talk to her.

The three of us entertained ourselves throughout the afternoon, walking around the yard, talking, whatever we did. At one point, we started talking about 25-cent words, and I reveled in my ability to rattle off 4- and 5-syllable tongue-twisters and to use them in actual sentences.

I found I enjoyed spending time with Lita. Dylan was cool, too, but my emotions were in full swing, and it was pretty little Lita Ortiz who captured the lion's share of my attention. What I felt was not sexual. And I'm not even sure it was romantic, in the traditional sense, because I knew she was way too young for me at the time. Even so, I felt a distinct urge to be with her, talk to her, listen to her, an excitement when she was near, a loss when she was distant.

I told my new friends about Erika, at least an abbreviated version of the story, with enough detail elided such that all they knew was: she was a girl whom I liked, and we had fought, and I had said some things I regretted, and I wanted to make up with her. I also showed Lita the letter I had been writing to Erika. The details of what happened next have been lost to time, but I've been able to reconstruct part of it. Through an accident, involving Lita, my letter was all but destroyed in the process. Certainly, it could not be salvaged.

I was livid with Lita, and I railed at her, that she also was "an obnoxious, self-centered, egotistical, dirty, little, two-faced slime ball."

While I stayed over at Dylan's that night, he asked me whether I liked Lita, and I told him, "a little." But I really meant "a lot, a whole big lot." He told me how he and Lita wrote to each other. So he and I exchanged addresses so that we could keep in touch, and he also gave me Lita's address, so that I could apologize to her. It was the first of numerous apologies, as we became long-term pen pals.

Meanwhile, Erika and I ended it, whatever "it" was, and I admitted defeat. Looking back, I wonder what I was trying to win that I could be defeated. I'm sure Erika ultimately made some man a wonderful partner, but at the time, she had been unavailable to me, and I knew as much. Remember, our whole relationship had started with what was clearly a joke. We still considered each other friends, however, and we prom-

3. The Blonde in the Pink Sweater

ised to write.

Friday night, May 29, 1984, I had a dream about Erika. We were at a party together. We entered an underground passage, which was equipped with an alarm that was set off whenever someone moved any of the lever-shaped doorknobs. We accidentally set off the alarm and became trapped in the passage, as guards started charging at us from all directions. I grabbed Erika's hand and whisked her away to safety.

I put my arm around her and told her I loved her, but she just giggled. I said, "I understand," and rested my hand on her knee.

Then she was kissing little children. Someone observed that if a child wanted a kiss from Erika, he would put his arm around her. So I waited until we were alone, then I put my arm around her and said, "What do I have to do for a kiss?" She was a very good kisser. I wanted to write her an apology for all the mistakes I had made. Then I woke up.

Knowing what I know now, the dream was probably not about Erika at all. Rather, Erika probably stood in as a metaphor for someone else I had been thinking about that day. However, at the time, I woke up with thoughts of Erika.

I actually wrote to Erika, even though we lived nearby, and told her all about the dream.

In December of that year, we moved out of state, to

the Boston area, where I remained into adulthood. I wrote Erika again, and she wrote back wishing me a happy holiday season, and urging me to stay in touch. But we quickly fell out of touch.

A year and a half later, in the summer of '86, she wrote me once more. She said there were so many things we had left unsaid, so many things she wanted to ask me. I agreed. I wrote back, a rambling letter urging her to please write, or even better, to call. Maybe instead I should have written about school, about my plans for college, about classes, about AP calculus, anything to lighten the mood. But I didn't think about any of those things, because I so wanted to talk to her.

I don't ever remember hearing from her again, and I didn't even attempt contact until many, many years later.

4. The Sister I Never Had

When I first met Lita Ortiz, she was only 11½, and I was a month from turning 15. I sensed the significance of that difference.

We promised to write, and we did write. A long-distance relationship though it was, she was really a friend. At least I considered her a friend. In my letters, I shared with her the details of my life, especially the boring ones. And she was always sweet enough to write back, no matter how boring I had been in my previous letter.

So unlike me, Lita was outgoing and full of spirit, while I was quiet and withdrawn. She was a natural people person, eager and full of enthusiasm, effortlessly fostering new friendships. Meanwhile, I thought in concepts and facts, introspective, sensitive, deep. She was Phineas to my Ferb.

She revealed to me that after I had told Dylan that I liked her "a little," that he had forwarded that information on to her. I didn't hold it against either of them. She said that if I had known her longer, I probably wouldn't have called her a slime ball. And she said that she missed me.

I missed her, too. I enjoyed writing to her, but not only from friendship, also from affection, the kind a boy would feel towards a girl, and maybe even the kind of affection a brother would have for a sister. But regardless of how else I felt, I always had a crush on Lita, and would always have a crush on her. All us boys, we all had a crush on Lita Ortiz.

Since my father was a denominational officer, we attended the national convention. So did Lita, and she and I hung out together at the hotel where we both were staying. Each moment in her presence was joy and satisfaction; each moment leaving her, longing and sadness.

We strolled along the balcony overlooking the pool at night, a romantic sight, the pool in which we had just hours earlier been swimming. At one point, she placed her hand on my shoulder. Her mother happened to see, however, and took her aside for a mother-daughter talk, telling her that she shouldn't touch a boy like that, because he might get the wrong idea and think that she likes him. She relayed this to me with a dismissive tone, as though it were no big deal. I nodded understanding, but inside, my heart sank just a little.

We also—she and I along with her siblings and cousins—took to riding the elevators up and down to pass the time, a little game that hotel management

4. The Sister I Never Had

took unkindly to. One of the hotel staff, a large, imposing man, very quietly and politely told me to stop doing that. I guess when you tower over someone at three times his weight, you don't need to shout in order to be heard. I immediately found Lita and the rest of the group, got her attention by wrapping my arm around her shoulders, and gently told her the game was off, by order of hotel management.

Afterward, I remembered how natural it felt to have touched her in that way. There was nothing romantic about it. But it was affectionate, with the same affection I would have shown a younger sister, had I had one, the same affection I now feel toward my sisters-in-law.

Growing up in a household filled with boys, I didn't know what it was like to have a sister. I didn't know how to feel toward a sister. Since then, I've gained two daughters and four sisters-in-law, and I've realized that Lita probably thought of me as a brother. But while there were times that I felt very much a fraternal bond to her, what I felt went beyond that. I desired attention and affection, to spend time with her, to talk to her, just to be near her and to know she cared about me. And this desire stemmed not only from friendship but also from romantic longing.

As convention weekend drew to a close, I felt an acute need to tell her, straight out, how I felt. We took a long walk down the hall of the 14th floor and back again. She patiently waited for me to unload what was on my mind, but I couldn't form the words. I didn't even know what words to use.

Oh that I could go back and put words in my own mouth! I would tell her how special she was to me, how much I enjoyed spending time with her. I would tell her that I had never before met a girl who made me feel as welcomed and comfortable as she had or had been a better friend to me than she had that weekend. I would tell her how much I valued her friendship, but that even though I also had a crush on her, I realized that we were in different places, and it would never change how much I loved her or how much I valued her company, no matter where our lives led us.

Instead, I eventually let it slip, awkward and unseemly, that I liked her. She was clearly upset. And when her siblings and cousins got wind of what I had said, they taunted her about it. Despondent that I might be losing her, I desperately tried to make up with her, to try to smooth things over, but she didn't want to talk. Incensed, I tried to intrude my way back into her sphere of attention, which only made the situation worse.

At one point, she was helping to babysit a number of small children, while their parents were at meetings. I wanted to talk about why she was mad at me. She

4. The Sister I Never Had

insisted that she wasn't mad at me, but said she simply didn't have time to talk just then. Lita escaped from the lighted hallway into the dark room where the children were watching *Dumbo*, but I followed. She sat down on one of the chairs, lined up in rows for the children and childcare staff to sit on. Timothy Mouse had just brought Dumbo to visit his mother, and the choir began singing "Baby Mine." I sat down next to Lita, watching the movie, listening to the music, watching her. She stared straight ahead and ignored me, and in the flickering light, I saw upset and anger etched into her once glimmering countenance. Her once smiling cheeks had turned to stone. I eventually left.

To this day, that scene from *Dumbo* makes me feel like crying a little, because it reminds me of her and makes me feel sad.

Before we left for home, however, I demanded a picture. I chased her with a camera until she capitulated, stopped running and posed in the hotel hallway and allowed me to take a snapshot, just to get me off her back. That snapshot, despite the look of exasperation in her eyes, on her face, is the only photo I still have of Lita, and one of my most cherished memories from my youth.

I wrote to her and told her I was sorry for the misunderstanding, that I thought of her as a friend and a friend only, and that I had been wrong to have butted my nose into her business. As usual, she accepted my apology, and she apologized herself for overreacting, and we began writing again.

But this experience for me had an unfortunate side effect. When you share your feelings and you get hurt for the trouble, you're less likely to share the same feelings next time. So the experience further ingrained the inclination, when I felt attracted to a girl, to keep my feelings to myself, to introspect about my feelings instead of sharing them with the person who might return them. I became even more scared of rejection and even more prone to obsess, instead of acting on my feelings and dealing with them effectively.

None of this was Lita's fault, of course. She did nothing wrong. She never deceived me or wronged me, nor did she ever lead me on. I simply had an unshakable crush on Lita Ortiz. It was my own bad timing, one of those "sometimes life sucks" moments. We were in two different places. I simply wanted more from the relationship than she was able to give.

As the years went on, we wrote less and less frequently. I saw her in 1988 and heard her sing for the first time, with a voice that challenged the angels', and standing there looking as beautiful as ever. But she had less and less time for me.

Even so, to the very end, I always opened my letters to her with "Dearest Lita," and I meant it.

4. The Sister I Never Had

Lita has always occupied a special place in my heart. Now, it's the same place my sisters-in-law also occupy, because they're part of my family, and my family is the most important thing in my life. It's something I can't explain logically. I was overjoyed when I was able to reconnect with her after 22 years, as spunky and as beautiful as ever, just recently married and all smiles. And it all made me smile, too.

5.   The Crushes Between

My pattern was that I would only develop feelings for girls who were unavailable, emotionally or romantically. The less available, the better. Some of the girls I showed interest in had their own problems. They were looking for quick fixes to their loneliness or a support system. Sometimes, they didn't know what they wanted. But more usually, they simply didn't know that I existed, or if they did, that I was interested in them. And then I usually wouldn't tell them about how I felt until after I had introspected about it to the point that it became creepy, which would be sure to pique their interest—negative interest.

This strategy had the effect of making my heart feel like it was being crushed in a vise. And other than that, all it served to accomplish was to make me feel miserable.

I had a crush on this one girl in school: short, black hair; pale skin; blue eyes; daughter of one of the teachers (whose class I did not take); and as popular as they come. So out of my league, but that didn't matter:

5. The Crushes Between

remember, the less available, the better. Eventually, I mustered the courage to ask her out, or whatever served as the closest analogue in ninth grade back then.

She turned her face so that I wouldn't see her giggling and said, "I'm sorry." Giggle. "I can't—" Giggle. She shook her head. "I just can't."

"I understand." I replied, but I actually didn't.

Over the years, I got discouraged. I never did get the American dating system. I finally decided not to bother with girls, if you believe my journals from that time.

Then I developed a crush on a "tasty morsel" (as one of my friends once described her), Priscilla, a tiny, light-haired brunette with a slim figure and freckles, one of the prettiest girls around. We became casual friends. We went to the same high school and both intended to go on to become engineering majors in college. We also attended the same church, and she was one of the first people I met when my family had moved into the Boston area. She washed her hair, it was rumored, two or three times a day (probably an exaggeration), and she enjoyed watching sports on TV.

Priscilla knew how I felt about her, I am sure, but she pretended not to. She told me about her boyfriend, with a smile and a lilt of satisfaction in her voice. She may have even taken some perverse pleasure in reminding me that I could not have her. Whatever her motives or actual feelings, I experienced the same depression that I had felt when I had noticed Maryanne smiling at another boy.

Eventually, I washed my hands of her, but before that, I had written one more poem full of sweet, passionate words celebrating our relationship and pledging forever. Given the situation, in retrospect, I have to wonder—and maybe this is bitterness talking, but... What the hell was I smoking?

In another case, years later, I developed a crush on this girl, a little young for me, but her mother liked me and trusted me. We sat and talked sometimes. She was small, cute, with dark hair framing a small, pale face dotted with freckles. She had her problems, including an absentee father, as I recall, but mostly she was normal, though sometimes sad.

Once, she was being chased by a group of guys in the church building where we both attended services. Whether they were teasing her or assaulting her I wasn't sure, but she definitely didn't want to be chased, and she seemed frantic to get away from them. Her little brother was with her, and I secreted them in one of the Sunday School rooms and locked the door.

The idea was to pretend that the room was empty. But she was in a panic, afraid of being caught. I gently said, "Now, settle down," and immediately she stopped her anxious rambling and began to stare into my eyes.

5. The Crushes Between

She was standing with her back against one of the walls, while I stood over her, my hand braced against the wall above her shoulder. We held our breath. All was silent. I experienced one of those charged moments, in which we felt so close. I wasn't sure whether I should kiss her. I wanted to, to kiss her and hold her. And I probably would have, if it weren't for her little brother standing in the room with us.

We did date, one time. I asked her what she wanted to do, and she said she wanted to go rollerskating. Okay. It didn't matter to me that I sucked on roller skates—still do. But what was I thinking? (Answer: I wasn't.) After making a sufficient fool of myself, and losing her to the crowd of real skaters, I asked her if she'd like to get a bite to eat, something I was much more adept at. But she had apparently met someone else at the rollerskating rink and wanted to spend some time with him. I was livid, demanded we leave immediately, drove her home, angrily. As I recall, she claimed we had not been on a date—and maybe she really did believe that—but I wasn't going to hear it. We didn't talk anymore after that.

Of course, I didn't always do it wrong. During my sophomore year in college, I met a voluptuous high school senior who was about to graduate. We met through a mutual friend. Long, loose black waves wrapped a pretty face. She wore a little too much makeup for my tastes, but she seemed nice, and I could imagine us having something together. I wrote her a lighthearted letter, talking about how different college will likely be for her than high school was, talking about my field of study and asking about hers, passing along a brief message from our mutual friend, and asking her to write back. I never heard from her again, and her memory dissolved unceremoniously into the bottom of my memento box. If I were to have repeated that experience with every girl I liked, I would have been much happier as a teenager and young adult, but unfortunately, she was the exception, and the rule was much more painful.

Too many girls, too many crushes. I remember most of the names and faces, but few of the details. But the feelings were always the same, as was the paradigm.

6. On Again, Off Again

We rode up to Monadnock Bible Conference for a Christian youth retreat in early 1985, me in the front passenger's seat, Priscilla and her sister in the back. We didn't arrive until after dark. At one point, I looked back and saw Priscilla napping, her head leaning gently against the car window. We had bundled up for the cold weather, even though the car was reasonably warm inside, and she was cuddled up inside her winter coat, resting peacefully. I took a few moments to admire how perfectly beautiful she looked in the moonlight.

During the weekend, I spent an inordinate amount of effort trying to find ways to be near Priscilla. I'm sure I annoyed her to no end, even though I knew that there could be nothing between us. But I finally did get a snapshot of her and her sister before we left back for home.

Then an unexpected switch. One of the girls there, one of my friends, told me about a girl named Peggy, who liked me.

I shook my head. "Who's that?"

So-and-so's sister.

Blank stare.

"Kind of tall?"

Nope. Nothing.

"Dark hair?"

Oh! Dark *hair*. Well, that narrows it down.

"She's in *that* car over *there*."

So I finagled a way to ride back sitting next to Peggy.

I had never had a girl genuinely like me like that, at least not that I knew of. In retrospect, there were probably plenty of girls who liked me, or who might have liked me, if I had given them the chance, but I never paid them any notice. But I instinctively knew that I would enjoy being in a relationship with a girl who actually did like me, for a change. I may have been an idiot, but I was not stupid: I was learning.

I sat in the car next to Peggy, in the back seat, she on the right, I in the middle. I placed my arm on the car seat behind her shoulders. All smiles, Peggy turned to look at our friend through the rear window: thumbs up.

Peggy's father clearly had a good job, because they lived in a nice house in a nice neighborhood in the suburbs. Their basement den housed a TV and a pinball machine. And her father was a fan of the Commodore 64, as was I. He also had loads of

6. On Again, Off Again

Commodore 64 games, which he was all too happy to share with me.

Peggy and I both being teenagers, we hung out together at church youth events at my father's church in Norwood, MA. When the youth group went roller-skating—and you may remember, I sucked on roller skates—I shuffled out onto the floor next to Peggy, desperately trying to keep my balance, hanging on for dear life.

Suddenly, she said, matter-of-factly, "Okay, there's a limit."

At first, I didn't know what she was talking about. Then I noticed that I was steadying myself with my hand on her breast.

Embarrassed, I moved my hand, apologizing profusely. I hope she believed me that it was just an accident, and I hope she had a good chuckle from the incident.

All in all, It was nice to have a girl to spend time with, someone who liked me and accepted me, someone I could be myself with. When I cracked a stupid joke, she got it, and she even laughed occasionally. And it was fun to sit next to each other in church, or to smooch in the corner where no one could see us, even to have the youth leaders keep a special eye on us to make sure we weren't getting into trouble.

Peggy had also had some sad and traumatizing

experiences in her life, the details of which I don't wish to go into. She and her brother were adopted, and her younger sister was her parents' natural child. I always got the sense—whether I was right or wrong—that Peggy felt inferior to her sister, as though her parents played favorites.

She went to a special, private school. I visited once or twice, at special events, and met the diverse and unusual cast of characters who were her friends. I see now that these people were her life, because she was so excited to have me meet them, to show me off. She obviously cared very much about them and was very proud to have me there next to her. But at the time, all I could think was how much of an outsider I was, how much I failed to connect with them, and I blamed it on them, because they were strange to me, because they were not like me.

After a while, the relationship fizzled out. No fighting. No fanfare. No going-away party. No divorce decree. No big, white, goodbye cake. I simply broke up with her. I don't even remember how I did it, what words I used, or exactly what reason I gave. I just did it. I knew it would make her feel like shit. I did it anyhow.

Years later, in 1990, after I had gotten over Enola (see chapter 7, "A Search for Meaning"), I ran into Peggy again. By that time, I had quit college, my father

6. On Again, Off Again

had started a new church, which met in Islington. The family had moved to Walpole, and I was there with them, trying to figure out what to do with my life.

I was also tired of being lonely again, so I asked Peggy out again, and we began dating again.

She introduced me to her new friends, and I introduced her to mine. My best friend Dave and Peggy and I frequently hung out at Bickford's, an eggs-and-pancake chain restaurant, eating a late supper (or extremely early breakfast, depending on how you look at it), drinking coffee from a bottomless cup, playing the video games in the foyer. Dave and Peggy became chummy-chummy with some of the waitresses there—they were always better at that than I.

Up until that time, my knowledge of sex was limited to almost nothing. Back in Sharpsville, in study hall one day, a group of guys congregated around my desk with a dirty magazine. Horny teenage boys, we were fascinated by the female body, a distinctly different desire than romantic longings. I didn't want to be with these women. I didn't care who they were. I didn't want to talk to them or get attention from them. I felt no affection for them. I just wanted to see them naked in provocative poses.

That experience characterized the extent of my practical sexual education.

Between then and 1990, I had heard and read bits

and pieces. I may even have caught some discussion about sex on one of the old computer BBS's that predated the Internet. But mostly my thoughts and feelings about sex were just what I imagined in the ignorance of my own mind.

I had no practical education in the subject. I kept my animal desires under control using the Joycelyn Elders solution. Yes, she eventually lost her job by foolishly advocating it. But let's admit: at least for me, the solution basically worked.

One evening, Peggy and I arrived at Bickford's a little early. We sat in my old, brown Dodge Aires, which was old when I had bought it to get to and from my college classes. We kissed for a while. And kissing turned into necking. And necking turned into petting. And petting turned into exploring. We both knew it wouldn't go any farther than that—or at least *I* knew. I kept my virginity. But it was fun, and it was the first time I had really explored the sexual side of love.

Peggy was at my 21st birthday party, and she gave me a cute and funny birthday card, which I still have. She loved me for who I was, but as before, I began to doubt her and lose faith in our relationship.

One evening, for example, on the way to meet Dave, she asked me to stop off at her girlfriend's house. She needed to stop quickly, she said, to pick up something she had lent out. It was an emergency, but she'd only

6. On Again, Off Again

be a minute. I stayed in the car and waited for her. A half-hour later, I started wondering what was taking so long. I found her inside chewing the fat with her girlfriend. Apparently, she had a personal problem—I never found out what—that she didn't feel comfortable discussing with me, but she couldn't get to her girlfriend's house to discuss it with her without a ride from someone, a someone who turned out to be me. It seemed to me that she'd had no intention of being only a few minutes.

I didn't get why she hadn't just asked me to drop her off at her girlfriend's, so that I could go on to meet Dave. I didn't get why she had lied to me. But mostly, I didn't get why she was afraid to share her life with me. I was supposed to be her boyfriend, yet she seemed to hide from me what she thought and felt, even to cover up the tracks that might lead me to the real Peggy. She accepted me the way I was, but she couldn't trust me to accept her the way she was?

So even though I had companionship and attention and affection, I still ended up feeling empty. Eventually, I ended up breaking up with Peggy again, despite fearing how hard she might take the breakup.

Many years later, I connected with Peggy again, and discovered that she had survived, as I had. But I always felt sorry that I had, in my quest for companionship, broken up with her—not just once—but twice.

7. A Search for Meaning

She bought a Bob Seger CD; I bought *Neil Diamond's Greatest Hits*, because I wanted to listen to the song "Hello, Again." I had met her through one of Dave's friends, and she felt like my first crush all over again.

It was 1989, and I was 19 going on 20, and she stared up at me through deep brown eyes and delicate, gold-rimmed glasses, from a sensitive and quiet heart, and she smiled dimples like sun rays in a sky freckled with starlight. She had dyed her blonde hair golden red, and it suited her.

Enola made me appreciate the beauty of red hair.

And she had a bad back, and I foolishly like an absent-minded jerk always hugged her too hard.

But what I remember most about Enola is what I learned while she was in my life. If spirituality is the search for meaning, we may both have been on the same journey. I was surely searching for meaning in life and relationship. I don't know that Enola helped me find it, but just by being there, she did urge me to look.

7. A Search for Meaning

She knew Dave and I were religious. That is, we went to church, and we studied the Bible, and having been the pastor's kid and raised in the church, I knew my Bible and what it said and—just as importantly—what it *didn't* in fact say. And I guess Enola also knew that Dave and I accepted her the way she was, because when her brother asked her to visit his church, she asked *us* to come along, for moral support.

I only remember bits and snippets: singing hymns at a Bible study in a lecture hall, no instruments but oh what inspiring voices; a service in a church sanctuary filled with oaken pews; hearing a band from the church play, awed by the drummer who bounced his stick off the hi-hat at over 360 taps a minute; visiting Enola's brother at his apartment, and his neighbor yelling at me for parking in front of the wrong house; arguing biblical doctrine and practice with him, and hearing him say that I clearly had my mind made up, as he decided not to waste any more time on me.

Throughout all of this, however, I never really established what Enola was thinking. I knew she was empty inside. I knew she had been through a bad experience, although I didn't know what it was. I rarely remember her smiling. She seemed to want a change, but probably didn't know what. She may have felt unloved or without direction. Or maybe I was the one who felt unloved and without direction, and I was reading my own feelings into her reactions.

I had immediately been taken with her, but I knew she was in no position to return my affections. All I could do was to be the best friend I knew how, which probably wasn't a very good one, because I was so wrapped up in my own feelings.

A group of us went to see Whiteheart perform, and Kim Hill opened for them. I had never heard Kim Hill's music before, her folksy Christian rock. The PA volume was loud, so loud that it rung in my ears, but I enjoyed her music anyhow and became a fan. When Whiteheart came out, however, and the sound guys seemingly turned up the volume even more to blasts of heavy-metal guitar, I exited the hall, escaped to the foyer.

Dave and Enola were also there, hiding from the harsh tones that were destroying the eardrums of the rest of the audience inside. Enola stared out of a window blankly, out into the darkness, seemingly at nothing in particular. Dave reached over and massaged her neck with his hand. I did not know what she was thinking, but I felt sad for her.

I was searching for meaning in romance, and I thought religion might provide it. I read book after book, bought from the local Christian book store, in an attempt to understand the feelings I had. Looking again at some of those books now, I see that the answers I needed were right in front of my face. But I

7. A Search for Meaning

didn't see them, because I was asking the wrong question. I was asking how to get the girls I loved, rather than how to find a girl who would love me back.

Ironically, I should also have been exploring the Harlequin Romance shelves at the local Barnes & Noble, or the slightly less-cheap mass-market paperback romances, or even the more expensive literary romances: anything that would have demonstrated to me the art of romance, as well as the science of love. But at the time, I was a fact-driven creature, and this was how I learned.

One book made a particular impact on me, *Caring and Commitment: Learning to Live the Love We Promise* by Lewis B. Smedes. In my search for the meaning of love, this was my enlightening, my revelation, my key, my Rosetta Stone. This was what I had been looking for all those years, a commitment. I had always cared, about every girl I had ever liked and every girl I had dated. But I had not secured a commitment, or even offered one. It made sense.

This concept was not idiotic. But what I did with it was.

My feelings had already boiled over and were bubbling out of the pot and all over the stove. So I channeled them into a promise, one-sided though it was. I started to spend more time with Enola, sometimes driving great distances to see her. I was already thinking about her almost all the time. She began to say that she wanted to meet with me, but she just didn't have time. Once, I drove to the McDonald's where she worked, during her shift, and opened with a lame crack: "So, this is the lunch rush?" She did not laugh and didn't have time to chitchat. Maybe I ordered some fries before I left. I wrote in my journal, "I love you. I will always love you... because I said I would. But why must you make me cry?"

By the way, this was not exactly what Lewis B. Smedes had advocated in his book.

Around that time, Richard Marx had recorded a new hit song, "Right Here Waiting":

> Wherever you go, whatever you do,
> I will be right here waiting for you.
> Whatever it takes, or how my heart breaks,
> I will be right here waiting for you.

That song stuck with me. A few years later, I was out with a bunch of friends, including a guitarist friend, who began to play the lead to that song on his 6-string acoustic. Before he even got a single line out, I asked if he could please not play that song.

"Why not?" he asked.

"It reminds me of somebody," I told him.

An understanding guy, he sympathized and jammed on something else instead.

Eventually, Enola and I faded out of contact.

8. The Heartbreak Girl

I usually didn't develop feelings for blondes, but there were exceptions. One I met through one of my friends, Ed, when he brought me into his group of friends. We all hung out sometimes, went to a young-adults church group on Friday nights, played pool, ate out, whatever. By this time, we were all young adults, but we still thought of ourselves as "girls" and "boys."

Mandy was not the prettiest girl in the world, but she struck me as loving, caring, and sensitive. When I met her, I had convinced myself that women were all just looking to have their own desires met—physical pleasure, money, prestige, or whatever—without giving a hoot for the deeper needs of their partners. On the verge of an emotional depression, I was ready to give up on love.

Then I met Mandy. Of all the people in Ed's group of friends, she was the only one who said "Hi" to me. She then instructed Ed to introduce me to everyone, something he must have thought was unnecessary. She smiled back at me when I smiled at her. She made me feel welcome.

Of course, she was also dating someone pretty steadily, and I had no desire to challenge that relationship. But then it ended, and I found it more and more difficult not to see her as a potential girlfriend. She was studying to be a professional chef, and when she got a brand new wok as a gift, she liked it. When I got my new Chevy Beretta, she was so excited, she just *had* to drive it. And so of course, I let her.

I finally told her, as tactfully as I could, how I felt about her. But she simply did not feel the same about me. My heart was crushed, but I held in the tears so as not to make her feel guilty or uncomfortable.

As Dave told me, though, there was always hope. And that hope carried me through, kept me searching for the attention and affection that I so desperately needed, even if I was going about it the wrong way. Ironically, this hope and the zeal it inspired were both healthy responses to my heartache, because they kept me from falling into depression. I ached, but as long as I was trying to win Mandy's heart, I never gave up.

By the middle of March 1991, I had sent Mandy several cards, but she never answered or mentioned them.

At that time, I actually had feelings for both Mandy and Helena. Helena was my best friend Dave's sister. When I had first met her, I had naturally been attracted by her long, dark hair and blue eyes, but I

8. The Heartbreak Girl

reasoned that it was just a passing crush. The situation was complicated by the fact that she was my best friend's sister, although I don't think he would have held it against me if I had dated her. Even so, as we hung out and talked, I began to get to know her, and I actually started to care about her.

I talked to one of my friends at work about them. I guess I just needed someone to talk out my feelings with. She quickly advised me that if Mandy hadn't mentioned the cards that I had sent, she wasn't worth my time, and that I should forget about Helena, because it was a touchy situation. In retrospect, good advice, very good advice.

Helena didn't believe in dating friends, for fear of losing the friendship. True, our friendship was not yet as close as some I had previously had, but it was close enough that we both had reason not to want to endanger it. I also had a feeling that she didn't feel the same way about me as I felt about her, maybe because that had been the pattern in my life, or maybe because she really didn't.

I decided not to mention my feelings to her. But the ultimate reason was not because I thought it was a bad idea. I didn't want to reveal to her how I felt, because I was afraid of being rejected... again. I was sick and tired of being rejected, and I was deathly afraid of it. Each rejection, I wrote in a diary entry, was another stomp, pushing my heart further into the ground.

Mandy, on the other hand, we reacted and felt similarly, even if our experiences had been quite different. I empathized with her and cared about her deeply, even though she sometimes sounded as though she were all alone. I thought—and still do—that she was a lovely person, and I planned to be on the other end of the tunnel, waiting for her with a light. If she had offered her heart to me, I would have accepted, unconditionally.

On the other hand, I was a desperately lonely guy, who felt completely alone in his own profound loneliness. At root, I simply wanted a girlfriend, someone to love, someone to spend time with, someone to attend to and also to show me attention, someone to return my affections. And I was convinced—quite rightly—that there would always be an unfilled void in my heart, until she arrived.

I finally got in touch with Mandy and asked her to do something with me, not a date, just an outing. I wanted to get close to her, to be involved in her life, to give myself a chance with her. We made tentative plans for Wednesday night, but she refused to commit. I understood that she was hurting from past relationships, and that she had other friends, but I also felt like an outsider to her, because she seemed to have less and less time for me.

8. The Heartbreak Girl

Come Wednesday, I called Mandy, as we had arranged, but she wasn't in. She had gone to her friend's house. I felt stood-up.

I finally got in touch with her. By that time, it was late, after 7:00.

"I miss you," I said.

"Oh... Thanks," she replied.

"What happened?"

She explained that after classes that day, her friend had asked her over, and she needed to study for an important exam the following day. She told me all about it.

"Anyway," she explained, "it's not like I blew you off or anything."

True enough, because she had not committed to going out with me Wednesday. She only suggested we talk and see whether things worked out. But I had been looking forward to spending time with her.

"It sure seems that way to me," I said.

"It's not like we had definite plans or anything."

"Except that I was going to call you."

She told me that she didn't mean to be unavailable, but that she had lost track of the time.

Looking back, I understand how she felt, and I understand what she did, and I agree with her priorities. But at the time, I felt like I was at the bottom of her list, and that sucked.

I bought her a card, with hearts on the front the loveliest shade of lavender, and the words: "Over and over, Time and time, Again and again... I find myself thinking of you." Inside, I wrote: "Just a reminder to let you know that there is someone who cares about you, is thinking about you, and isn't about to forget you."

I asked Dave to deliver it, along with a single, long-stemmed, red rose. He did, the following Sunday.

When I called later that night, she said, "I got the rose you sent. Thank you."

Then she explained that she didn't feel the same way I did, and she didn't want to lead me on by seeing me too much. She didn't understand how I could care so much, why she meant so much to me, and she didn't know whether she could trust me.

I argued with her for a time, listing reasons why I should care for her and why she should trust me. The one reason I didn't think of, which might have even been the ultimate clincher, is that I simply did. Just as Christ, it is said, had no reason to love us, but he nonetheless came to Earth as a man and delivered grace on our behalf, so also I had no good reason to care so deeply about her; I just did.

But she just didn't feel anything for me, and she felt we didn't have anything in common, and so she believed a romance just couldn't work between us.

Of course, neither did Dave and I have anything in

8. The Heartbreak Girl

common, and that didn't keep us from intimacy. Even though I was an idiot, one thing that was *not* idiotic was my belief in love and commitment. Even then, I knew that common interests were insubstantial next to a common bond, which is really what makes or breaks a relationship. As an old, married man now, I know that while feelings can push you into the arms of a lover, they cannot make love.

Ironic, however, that having felt that push myself, I was ready to deny it to Mandy.

She must have sensed my anguish, because she eventually told me she was not going to hurt me anymore by allowing me to be her friend. She may also have been afraid of being hurt herself by trying to be friends with a guy who was so taken with her.

And that, as they say, was that.

She was right, of course, in that there was no way we could have been only friends, as strongly as I felt.

Although I maintained intermittent contact with several of the members of that group of friends, I had been effectively excluded from it from that time forward.

Was it idiotic of me to pursue her, given that I felt as strongly as I did? Perhaps not. But in the grand scale, it was clearly idiotic of me to pursue girls that were clearly uninterested in being pursued.

9. Only Just Friends

I was a vulnerable child, longing for love.

In May 1991, Ed, Helena, and I, along with another of Ed's friends, visited Castle Rock, in Marblehead, MA. There I sensed that Helena was also in some ways a vulnerable child, longing for someone to love her. I ended up telling her about Maryanne, my first crush, the full and unvarnished version of the story. I surprised myself, because it was the first time I had ever shared the story with anyone. I don't know whether Helena realized how big an admission it was for me.

Having dropped everyone else off at home, and driven up to her house, we talked. I shared with her some of the angst I had been going through, and she supported me. Helena was a wonderful friend.

As we parted, I asked her to wait. "I have another unusual request to make," I said.

"What?" she asked.

"Give me a hug?"

She not only hugged me, she held me, wrapped her arms around me, gave me the human contact I needed,

9. Only Just Friends

just what I needed to make me feel better.

The next day, Memorial Day 1991, Ed and Helena and I hiked across Blue Hills. We packed a small lunch and some water, then we climbed Great Blue Hill and set out along the Northern Skyline. When we reached the road, we followed it south until we met the Southern Skyline, and hiked it back. Along the way we climbed and descended the gentle knolls and rocky hummocks, too many to count, until our legs ached.

We stopped for lunch in a clearing on one of Blue Hills' peaks. Helena and I argued about the definition of *chaos*, the kind of intellectual argument we frequently enjoyed together, while Ed sat between us.

Suddenly, Ed stood, walked as far as our little clearing would allow, and emphatically said, "I'm not getting in the middle of this!"

Something clicked inside me. I didn't feel our discussion was heated, nor did I feel it was going to be. Helena and I disagreed, yes, but it was a friendly disagreement, academic, over an insignificant matter. From my perspective, it was simply fun talk. We eventually agreed that only God could possibly make a universe so ordered, so predictable, yet so complex and unpredictable as ours, a fulfilling conclusion.

Afterward, we went over to Ed's house and watched *Ghost*, which I had never seen before, and *Waterloo Bridge*, starring Robert Taylor and Vivien Leigh, one of my all-time favorite unknown classic movies. *Ghost* made me cry, and as *Waterloo Bridge* closed, I glanced over to notice Helena wiping her eyes.

I suddenly noticed something about Helena. I had always admired her long, dark hair. But that night, I noticed that her eyes sometimes shone from beneath dark eyebrows, like sapphires. And delicate freckles dotted her nose and face. She was pretty, beautiful, but I said nothing, because I didn't want her to think I was off my rocker.

I wondered whether Dave knew how I felt about Helena. He had always seemed to notice, even before I did, when I was developing feelings for a girl. And this was his own sister!

I found myself loathing that every time Helena and I did anything together, Ed was always there with us. It was as if he was in the way. I enjoyed sitting next to Helena in church, when she came, because he wasn't there. And I cherished the experiences the two of us shared alone.

A wiser man would have gotten out as fast as he could, gotten as far away as possible, because Helena didn't date friends, and she didn't date younger guys, and I was both. Of course, I was only younger by a miniscule amount, but that wouldn't have saved me from being her friend. I even knew all this at the time and had figured it all out, that I was doomed to heart-

9. Only Just Friends

break if I pursued her.

Damn friendship! Maybe I should have been mean to her when I had the chance.

Instead, I mentioned how beautiful she was, and in public, with other people listening. I guess it ticked her off.

I didn't know how to treat a woman, I wrote in my journal, and I didn't want to learn. I had thought it was intuitive, but it wasn't. No woman would want to teach me how to be nice. No woman would want to accept me for who I was. Every woman I had ever met only wanted for themselves, only thought of themselves. But I had needs too. I would no longer, I resolved, expect any more from the fairer sex, because they weren't capable of open-mindedness.

So much for hope. Bring on the depression.

Helena later explained that she didn't like it when I pointed out her blue eyes. And she didn't like the way I stared at her, as though I were undressing her with my eyes. On my honor, I had never, not once, undressed her with my eyes. But I did notice her beauty, and I guess I shouldn't have. I would never have noticed Ed's physique, so I shouldn't have noticed hers, either. The day we went to Castle Rock, the night we talked in her car, she had thought we had established the bounds of our friendship, and then I had overstepped those bounds.

"I'll work on that, then," I said simply, my heart sinking toward oblivion, my world crashing around me.

Even back then, though, I realized that I had not actually done anything wrong. In retrospect, I see that I was a perfect gentleman, bestowing appropriate complements, which most women—even platonic friends—would swoon to receive.

How then did I manage always to pick the ones who would end up ripping my heart to shreds?

I was angry and hurt at the way Helena had spurned me, and it was many years before I was able to forgive her. Ironic, that she refused to date me for fear of destroying the friendship, yet in the end, Helena lost my friendship specifically because she couldn't take that risk. In retrospect, she clearly valued our relationship, maybe even more than I did, because I now know she kept letters I had sent her, and probably journals of our times together, too. But for some reason I didn't know, she just couldn't date me. The breakup might have hurt her as much as it did me.

I wrote a letter to her, which I never intended to send, because it was meant merely to describe my own feelings to myself, not to communicate anything to her. In it, I said:

> If I seem to be closely linking platonic friendship and romantic relationship, it's because I am. They are, after all, essen-

9. Only Just Friends

> tially one in the same, springing from the
> same roots of affection, growing as two
> people grow closer together. True love
> cannot in fact exist without a stable friend-
> ship... I cannot be superficial or vain in my
> love, for to do so would be to go against the
> already existing ties I have with you.

That was not idiotic.

But I never stopped to think that maybe she had no one to love her because she didn't let anyone love her, and that she wouldn't love me, because she was too busy protecting herself from getting hurt. That may not have been what was actually happening inside her —her motivations were likely much more complicated than that—but it was certainly an obvious thought that would have kept me out of trouble, had I thought it at the time.

I never stopped to think that even though Helena never wronged me—after all, she had been forthright regarding what she wanted out of the relationship; she had neither deceived me nor expected that which I had not promised—I in fact was the one who had failed to put reasonable bounds on our relationship. I was only just learning that what I was asking for was quite reasonable, and that I should have insisted on it ahead of time, before either of us got in deep enough to get hurt. So I was still an idiot, but I was learning.

10. Ain't Nothin' But a Horn Dog

I lost my head a little bit the first time I met Delilah. She was a local DJ who hosted an adult-contemporary, nighttime call-in show in Boston, though she would eventually end up with a nationally syndicated program.

We first met when she visited my father's church for services in the summer of 1991. We talked a little about music, and she told me she was looking for Christian songs that would be appropriate for her show. She said we should get together sometime and go through some of my CD's, and I could help her pick out some songs. I was so excited, I rushed right home, picked out a bunch of CD's, and drove right over to her house. It was only then that I realized that she meant that *sometime* we should get together.

We did get together. She took me to visit the station. We drove her SUV into the parking garage of the Prudential center and headed up to the 14th floor, where I sat in the studio, watching her work. In between callers and songs, we would talk, just her and

10. Ain't Nothin' But a Horn Dog

me. It was an experience that we would repeat numerous times over the following months.

I called her Dee, a nickname that her friend Re had coined. When Dee had first moved into the neighborhood, Re welcomed her, helped her plant the garden, went camping with her, and shared life with her. They became close friends, and this is the Dee that I met, so I naturally called her by her given nickname. Still do.

Once, I complained that I simply wasn't funny and that I didn't talk very well, especially to girls. I always felt awkward, even among friends, hard to get to know, a hard person to learn to like. Dee countered—sincerely, I am convinced—that when I relax, I'm actually quite funny and fun to be with. I had never before actually felt like a nice person, not like that at least.

Meanwhile, Helena decided to go back to school, to move to a college in New York. It was something that she really wanted to do, and I was genuinely happy for her that she was pursuing a goal she wanted.

But I still had feelings for her, and she still hated it. She told me not to do it again, not to express my affections for her, "and if you can't handle it, maybe we should just be friends from a distance: 'Hello,' 'Goodbye,' and that's it." So I avoided her, which I guess she also hated.

After she went to college, we wrote to each other. I asked if there was a compromise solution, something that would allow her to be comfortable with me, while still allowing me to express my feelings toward a friend. Whenever I had tried simply to do what she wanted, I ended up becoming hurt. Even then, I understood that I was a person, and I had feelings, too, and she was supposed to be my friend, and I rightly wanted her sympathy, even if I could not have her empathy. And if that was impossible, we should just dissolve our friendship.

I ached, yes, but I finally was free, liberated. This was one of the first truly empowering stands I had ever taken in love.

She replied with a letter that left me thinking I had lustful thoughts, or at least thinking that *she* thought I had lustful thoughts. In reality, I didn't even know the meaning of the word *lust*.

As Dee and I drove home from the station one night, I told her about Helena and about Helena's letters. I don't remember what words I used, or what unfair impression of Helena I may have left her with. But I do remember what she said back to me.

She said, "There's nothing wrong with you."

That was the first time in a long time that I truly felt validated, that I could feel what I felt and not feel guilty for it, that someone—a woman, a female friend—accepted me for who I was without passing judgement, the first time in a long time that I felt I could talk to a

10. Ain't Nothin' But a Horn Dog

woman without needing to dig into a bunker and lob grenades at her to make her listen to me. It felt so good, not just to know I was doing the right thing, but to feel acknowledged and accepted. Dee had that affect on people.

She was constantly meeting new people via her call-in radio show, and many of them were searching for spiritual fulfillment. And when she met such people, she invited them to church. I too met a number of interesting people through Dee, and some of them I got to know and befriended and cared about.

Tracy was one such special person. I met her when she visited our church, fiery red hair, a cute smile, and a curvy swagger that made me a little uneasy.

After services one Sunday, I sang for Dee a song I had recently written, mostly during a trip to the radio station. She had inspired this song, entitled "Blue and Grey," after the color of Dee's eyes. Tracy had stayed over and listened, too, and after the song ended, she said, "Wow. That's the story of my life." I was flattered, and the complement did send me on a little bit of an ego trip.

In retrospect, I wonder whether Tracy was really just there by chance, or whether she was there to notice me. Because she did notice me— I'm not complaining; despite Dee's friendship, my self-esteem was still scraping through the gutter, and I needed the attention and appreciated it.

But Dee was right in something else she had said about me, that I didn't have a lustful bone in my whole body. Dee, it seemed, couldn't fathom that Helena thought I was undressing her with my eyes or had lustful thoughts about her. I was a virgin in more ways than one: not only a virgin of the body, but also of the mind, inexperienced in flirting, blind to the signals of sexual attraction. My feelings had been romantic, not erotic.

Tracy and I spent some time together, and we began to date. I visited her home church, as she had visited mine. We listened to music, and one particular Elton John song, I said, reminded me of her. She said, the song was *about* her. One evening, I was playing some of my old, corny music recordings for her, on a whim, and she made a crack about how bad they sounded. I understood, but that music was part of my past, part of me, and I have to admit, that stung a little. But mostly, we had fun together, the kind of comfortable attention I had always wanted, and from a sexually attractive woman I would never have seen myself going out with. She was Peggy and Erika combined, but this time without all the childhood bumbling and angst.

Instead, we had adult-sized bumbling and angst. Tracy had a past, and at the time, I did not understand the significance of that past. When I found out that she

10. Ain't Nothin' But a Horn Dog

had a baby daughter, I wasn't freaked out. Nor did I think through the implications. I didn't think through what a baby girl would mean to our relationship—I was so not ready to become a father figure, to anyone. I didn't think through how the baby's *father* might affect our relationship, or that he might actually be present in Tracy's life.

One night, we were over at her apartment watching *He Said, She Said*. We lay together on the couch, she in my lap, I with my arms around her. We fit together hand-in-glove. I felt as though she were a blanket, soft and warm and comfortable, as we allowed ourselves to be entertained by Kevin Bacon and Elizabeth Perkins throwing passionate insults at each other.

Just as the movie was reaching its climax, the phone rang. This is long before society had developed the *Gilmore Girls* rule about no answering the phone during the movie. So Tracy answered it. And as she spoke pieces of a half-conversation, she became agitated, then upset. I think it was her ex, and whatever he said to her really disturbed her. She asked me to leave and wouldn't discuss it. We never did get to see the end of the movie.

Saturday, November 30, 1991, I went over to Dee's house with a bunch of our friends. The weather was warm enough for us to congregate outside in the yard, probably one of the last moderate days of the season.

Re had canceled their scheduled skating trip that day in order to go dirt-biking, and Dee was concerned and on-edge about it. She would be happy when Re was back safe at home, but for the time being, she wasn't very much fun to be with. Still, we all stayed, and we ate, and we hung out, and we socialized. That's what it was like at Dee's house, friendly.

That night, I had a big date with Tracy. We dressed up, went out to a nice Italian restaurant, soft music, mouthwatering aromas, subtle lighting, cloth napkins. We sampled the escargot—I thought they tasted like garlic-butter gummy worms. We discussed proper manners for a proper restaurant such as this, and I stared into her eyes in the flickering candlelight.

After dinner, I drove Tracy back to my house, where she had met me and parked her car. The temperature had dropped as night had fallen, and my hands were cold. Tracy knew how to fix that, though. She placed my hands between her legs, underneath her skirt. I felt the sheer fabric of her hose against my skin. It wasn't warm. I didn't get it. This wasn't working at all. My hands were still cold.

I was a mental virgin, remember, and I didn't understand that this was supposed to be the one thing that leads to another. So we said goodnight, and I went up to my room and started getting ready to turn in.

Some minutes later, Tracy called in a panic, saying

10. Ain't Nothin' But a Horn Dog

that a large, dark figure was snooping outside her apartment. I didn't get that, because neither of us lived in a crazy or dangerous neighborhood. I told her that if she was really worried, she should call 911. But she begged me to come over as fast as I could.

When I got there, I found—surprise!—absolutely nothing. I didn't understand that this, too, was supposed to be the one thing that leads to another.

She begged me to stay awhile, until she felt better. We sat on her couch. The baby was sleeping upstairs. We cuddled together a while, and then one thing really did lead to another.

When I kissed her, I tasted lipstick mingled with her saliva. She groaned as I touched her, as we rubbed our bodies together, as I flitted my tongue across her nipples. Before I knew it, I was half naked, neither knowing nor caring how far we would go, as she touched me, pleasured me.

Suddenly, she stopped. Looked at me. Said, "What am I doing? I can't. You're the pastor's son!"

The next morning, my mother woke me before church, said that Dee had called the previous night while I was out. Re had been riding her dirt bike without a helmet, accelerating too fast, when she lost control and ran headlong into a tree. She had been killed instantly.

And I had been out, almost losing my virginity,

when Dee's call about her friend had come in.

That morning, I met Dee on the church porch. I fell into her arms in the cool, wet, new-December-morning air, and we cried together a little. I hadn't known Re that well, but I knew she was important to Dee, and I cared about Dee just as she had cared about me.

Later that month, on Friday the 13th, I attended the company holiday party. I took a date. The evening was not unlucky. I asked Dee to accompany me, not Tracy. I strolled in wearing a black felt fedora that I had bought on an outing with her. I was standing next to a classy, sexy, leggy blonde, not to mention a local celebrity. I introduced her to all my coworkers. We drank Coke-and-limes and may even have danced a little.

On the way back, in the car, she reached her hand over, touched me, and said, "Thanks for taking me instead of Tracy."

The following day, I wrote her:
> Delilah, you've taught me how to love again. You took my crushed and broken heart and let me be worth something. You let me be a man, finally. You let me feel good about myself and good about being with you, and I *finally* wasn't committing some great sin by it...
>
> Love has always been a sad thing for me.

10. Ain't Nothin' But a Horn Dog

    Most of all, thank you for taking time out of your life to spend with *me* and just me... It means a lot to me when you remember to invite me to your house, to parties, but it means so much more when you make time for *me*... These are the times that I enjoy the most... because I know I am with someone who really loves me.

    And, yes, best friends *are* included!

That last line was an allusion to a conversation we'd had, the details of which I now wish I had recorded in my journal.

11. A Transforming Thought

I also developed a crush on Delilah. Yes, she taught me to love again, but I still didn't possess the skills to use this newfound knowledge.

Dee told me I jumped into feelings for someone without knowing whether she could return them. I immediately took offense. How dare she criticize my feelings?! I felt she was threatening me as a person, as though she were dismissing the me who was me. (As though Dee would *ever* have dismissed me or belittled me.)

But part of me understood that she was right.

My father and I also had several frank conversations about such matters. I don't know whether he was looking for an opportunity to talk to me—maybe he realized that something was perpetually disturbing me. Or maybe I finally sought him out, an older, experienced, wiser man, who during his decades as a pastor had seen and helped more relationships than I could count.

At one point, he told me that I was like he was at

11. A Transforming Thought

my age. I did not date just for fun, but for keeps. I was looking for someone to marry, because what's the point of dating a woman if I wasn't planning on marrying her?

That word *marriage* stuck in my head. I had truthfully never considered marriage. I wanted love, yes. I wanted commitment, yes. I guess I did want marriage. So then why wasn't I looking for a woman who would make a good *wife* for me? Regardless of whether my feelings were valid—and I still believed they were valid, and indeed they were—they had been leading me astray. I could not think of one single obsession that I had recently had that was toward a suitable maiden. And that was the problem, wasn't it?

On top of that, Dad suggested that I wait a week or two after meeting a girl, to cool off before asking her out on a date, and to take that time to think about the situation rationally, rather than being swept up by my feelings. And if I asked her out, and she said yes, fine. But if she said no, no big deal, because there was no relationship to start with, and I could get out before my feelings got hurt.

I met Margaret in February 1992 at a Bible study. We talked. She looked young for her age; she was a little older than I had originally thought, but I didn't see how that mattered, because we were still part of the same generation, spoke the same language. She was studying to become a physical therapist, renting a room in a friend's house, and putting herself through school by working at UPS. Moreover, she seemed completely and undeniably normal, no debilitating past, no extreme neediness, no spiritual crises, no psychological disorders, no indication of any desire to "just be friends." And her hair was dark, and her eyes were blue-grey, and her nose was flecked with tiny freckles, and her name began with M and R.

She was wonderful and perfect, so naturally I had completely no interest in dating her.

But I had been here before. The girls I was most attracted to had always ended up hurting me, and terribly so. It may not have been their fault, but I still did get hurt, over and over and over again. I was sick and tired of that pattern, and I knew I wanted to break it.

So I asked for Margaret's phone number, and she gave it to me.

I waited a couple weeks before I called her to set up a date. Unknown to me, each day after school, she raced up to her room to check her answering machine. No messages.

Until one day, I did call, and I asked her if she'd like to go out, and she said she would. We went bowling, and I sucked at bowling (almost as much as I sucked at rollerskating), but Margaret didn't seem to hold it

11. A Transforming Thought

against me. We had fun anyhow. Then we saw a movie together at the theater down the street. Then we went out for a late dinner at Bickford's, not fancy, but comfortable.

I was developing some sort of bony prominence on one of my wrists, probably due to my poor posture at the computer at work. I wasn't really concerned about it, but I was curious. And since she was studying physical therapy, I showed her my wrist.

She gently held my hand, so delicately, so tenderly examined it.

I stared into her eyes and wondered if I could fall in love with this woman.

Helena and I were still exchanging letters, and I wrote to her, telling her about Margaret. But, I said, "I'm not sure I'm ready. I mean, sure, I *thought* I was, but just meeting her brought back many memories... I found myself longing again for the relationships I've had most recently, which of course isn't fair to Margaret."

I had been under stress, obsessing over my feelings, desperately wanting to put the desires of my past in the past, but not knowing how to do it. I was falling asleep late, waking up early. Unknown to me, I was on the fast track to a major depression.

Helena eventually wrote back and said, simply, "Stop looking for a catch, and I don't think Margaret is a mistake."

Before that could happen, though, I answered my own questions easily enough.

Margaret and I went out with a bunch of Margaret's friends. We all stopped to eat at a restaurant. As I sat across the table from Margaret, I noticed out of the corner of my eye one of the waitresses, a trim, fit, fair-skinned beauty, wearing a skimpy white outfit barely one notch above a bikini. I kept my eyes trained on Margaret's face. Good boy!

As I recall, Margaret asked if I liked the way the waitress was dressed. I shrugged my shoulders. Truthfully, she was probably fun to stare at, if I could do so with impunity. But I wasn't about to date a girl like that, and I certainly knew enough not to let it distract me from my date with Margaret.

(Definitely *not* idiotic.)

That night, I drove Margaret and her friend to the friend's house, where we had all met up to go out. Before Margaret and I parted, we sat in the car and talked. I turned off the engine, because we had been sitting there for so long.

Time to say goodbye, I asked, "Can I kiss you?"

"Yes," she answered.

And I leaned over and kissed her, a long, deep, passionate kiss.

Unknown to us, Margaret's friend was still spying

11. A Transforming Thought

on us from her darkened window, and our kiss soon became the hot gossip within her circle of friends.

On a soon-future date, at Pizza Hut, as we waited to be seated, I told Margaret, out of nowhere, surprising myself, that I thought we would be together for a long time. I didn't know where that came from; it just came out so naturally, because I felt so comfortable with her.

Then one morning, a week or two later, at 3 AM, we were parked on the street near the church. I was to drive her to her job at UPS, because she worked the early shift at 4. She didn't want to go into work, but it was how she was supporting herself, at least for the time being. She coughed and said she was also afraid she might have pneumonia, so we prayed that she would get better.

Unknown to me, she was thinking in the back of her mind how in love she was with me, and that if I were to ask her to marry her, she would say yes. A crazy thought, maybe, but not idiotic.

In the middle of the conversation, out of nowhere, I said, "Will you marry me?"

She replied, "Yes."

"That was easy," I said.

She beamed.

Where was the wooing? Where was the longing? Where was the unrequited love? Where was the conflict, the angst? Where was the fighting for her affections? Where were the desperate pleas for attention? Where was the catch? There was none. We were simply two people, both looking for a committed lover, and when we found each other, we decided to get married. That's it. No suspense. No romance. No fanfare.

That day at work, her mind was filled with thoughts. *What came next?* she wondered. She had just accepted a wedding proposal. This was new, and it was interfering with her concentration.

"What's wrong with you, Margaret?" one of the managers asked.

She told him.

"So he's your fiancé, then?"

She gasped. *How are we going to have a wedding? Oh no! Isn't it the bride's family who pays for the wedding?*

The manager said, "You should learn to stop talking about your personal life during work time."

As for me, I told no one, until Margaret and I together stopped by a jewelry store in the mall and spontaneously bought an engagement ring. That is, she picked it out, an estate ring that she immediately fell in love with—before then, I had not even known she liked antiques—and I bought it for her.

Then we started making wedding plans.

I still lived at my parents' house, and Margaret frequently came over on Saturdays. One weekend, after

11. A Transforming Thought

a snowstorm, she slept over. We folded out the sleeper-sofa into a bed for her, and I slept in my own room. We acted the part of a good, proper couple, as of yet unmarried, and right across the street from the church my dad pastored. The next morning, Sunday morning, I awoke and descended the stairs to greet my fiancée. But not being a morning person, I ended up instead cuddling up next to her on the sleeper-sofa, my nose snuggled into her cheek.

When my mother walked in... *Gasp! And on a Sunday morning! What if someone from church had walked in?!*

Okay already I'm up!

But I still remember lying next to my beloved, snuggling up next to her in the morning, the warmth and softness of her cheek, how comfortable I felt, how well we fit together. I still feel that way whenever I snuggle up next to her in bed.

My father agreed to officiate at our wedding. He also counseled us on what we could expect as a married couple. I took away from those sessions some invaluable rules for a successful marriage, from a man who had actually made his own marriage work:

"You will fight," he said. "No marriage is free of fights. Fighting is normal. Just make sure you fight fair. Don't make it personal. Don't tell your spouse what's wrong with her. 'You know what the problem with you is?' Don't do that. Instead, focus on expressing your own thoughts and feelings.

"Don't hit below the belt. Some couples dig up old wounds, old hurts that they can blame on the other person. That's not fair. This fight is about today, not about what happened in the past.

"And never shout, just to get in the last word, and then storm out of the room, because that cuts off communication.

"Foster communication. Always know that you can discuss issues with the other person. Don't judge each other. And be willing to give up what you want in order to give the other person what she needs."

Finally, he said, "Remove divorce from your vocabulary. And always promise to love each other, unconditionally. Not, 'I'll love you if...' but 'I'll love you,' period. Because once you do that, you'll have the safety to work through anything else you encounter."

Unconditional love, I realized, is the First Amendment of marriage.

The First Amendment to the U.S. Constitution guarantees freedom of speech, freedom of the press, freedom of assembly, and freedom to petition the government. Even if the government infringes on our other rights, it is said, we the people can still take action to have those infringements rectified, as long as we have our First Amendment freedoms. The First Amendment represents the freedoms that protect all

11. A Transforming Thought

our other freedoms.

In the same way, if you have unconditional love that gives you enough safety in your relationship to work out all the other stuff that pops up. All I needed was someone I could trust to love me unconditionally. And Margaret was that someone.

Helena wrote me another letter expressing concern that I was going too fast with Margaret. "Please remember," she said, "how easy it is to fall too fast and not see where it is you're going to land."

Jumping in without knowing where you're going to land, eh?

Recently, I was driving in my car, Margaret behind me in hers. I supposedly knew where I was going, and she was following me. In reality, I had a general idea, but when it came down to the details, I was winging it, just following the road signs in the direction in which I thought our destination lay. At one point, I worried about what would happen if I got lost. But then I looked in my rearview mirror, and I saw Margaret following behind me. And I realized that I didn't care whether we got lost, as long as we got lost together.

You see, that's what marriage is like. No matter how carefully you've planned your life, thought of every contingency, in order not to get hurt by love, you never actually know what the future holds. In the end, if you want any chance of being happy, you have to jump in with both feet, not knowing where you're going to land, but knowing that wherever that is, your lover will be landing there too, right along beside you.

Margaret and I held our wedding at a local church the afternoon of September 11, 1993.

Doesn't that suck, having your wedding anniversary on 9/11?

Hell, no! We were husband and wife years before the date had anything to do with terrorism, and long after the twin towers have been relegated to a footnote in classroom history textbooks, we'll still be celebrating our marriage on that day.

In other words, we have dibs! Bad things happen somewhere in the world every day, and I refuse to give up the celebration that day represents for Margaret and me. So the terrorists will just have to find another day of the year for their thing.

12. Happily Ever After

By the time I was in my latter 30's and I had started studying marketing, one of the first things I learned was not to pursue sales leads that were unlikely to pay off, because you end up spending more money trying to get those people as customers than you would earn from them in profit. Pursuing the wrong customers is wasteful and expensive. Yet, this is precisely what I had spent most of my drawn-out adolescent love life doing, pursuing the wrong girls, and ending up forlorn.

Giving and receiving love is a fundamental human need, because we all need to love and be loved. Moreover, the way God made us, we naturally seek to meet our needs. And when we can't meet our needs, unhappiness, depression, and even psychosis can result. Dysfunctional behavior, too, is simply when we try to meet our needs and fail. And in my case, I finally understood—almost 20 years later—why I had been so dysfunctional when it came to love. I also finally understood that the only choice I really had if I was not to end up lonely was to barrel through it, heartbreak and all, until I had finally learned the lessons that would finally allow me to succeed in my quest to be happy.

During my junior and senior year of high school, I had regular talks with my guidance counselor. She took an interest not only in my classes and college plans, but also in my personal life, my friends, my challenges, my thoughts, my feelings. And she supported me, despite what I put her through. I was a headstrong, snotty kid, and as I explained my thought process to her, I frequently made "quantum leaps," as she called them, in logic.

It's part of my intuitive personality, that I've always drawn very fast, broad conclusions based on little data. Much of the time, I can't explain why these conclusions are right—at least not until I think about it—but I still know I'm right. And when I possess expertise in the subject—such as software development or writing—I usually *am* right. That's because, inside my head, my mind is putting together decades of experiences, mistakes, study, and practice, in order to come up with an answer.

Shortly after I turned 17, my high-school guidance counselor sent me a letter, wishing me a good summer. In it, she wrote many things, including one comment that sticks out at me now, 23 years later:

> Obviously you're tired of feeling lonely and somewhat isolated in some circles and have

12. Happily Ever After

> taken positive steps to remedy the situation... As we have discussed before, when you work from your personal experiences, your perceptions are usually very accurate. It's when you project yourself into hypothetical situations that we see those quantum leap assumptions that create anxiety, tension, and fearfulness. I have every confidence in your ability to handle real situations as they arise. Life is a developmental process, and you have come a long way in a relatively short time.

They say it takes 10 years of practice to become an expert in something. If you want to be a software developer, for example, as I did, you start off green behind the ears, half the time designing software that doesn't work, and the other half, software that's impossible to maintain. If you keep improving your craft, however, you'll be a proficient developer after about 10 years, capable of giving sound advice to the next generation of young-whippersnapper green-behind-the-ears code slingers graduating from college.

I began getting interested in girls in 1982, when I noticed Maryanne sitting in front of me in Algebra class. I met Margaret in 1992. Maybe that's just how long it takes.

In my case, being a shy, reserved boy who spent

most of his time inside his own head, my first attempts at romance were obvious failures. I had to learn how to process what I was feeling. I had to learn how to talk to girls. I had to learn to flirt. I had to learn what I valued in a relationship.

But even after I had learned all that, I still linked romance to the feelings of loneliness and longing that I had felt with Maryanne and the girls who came after her. And each heartrending experience only set that perverse connection deeper in my instincts. As a result, I fell only for those girls who were most likely to make me miserable—because miserable is what I associated with love. My brain was working from past experience to draw conclusions but ending up at the wrong result. This then evoked strong emotions, which overwhelmed my mind, making it impossible for me to think straight. As much as I wanted to be happy, I always ended up repeating the same pattern that saddened me and made me cry. A man who is ruled by what he feels has a fool for a master.

I didn't understand that while there was nothing wrong with how I felt, how I responded to those feelings itself affected how I would feel. That is, as psychologists have increasingly realized, not only does how you feel affect your what you do, but also does what you do affect how you feel. Studies have shown, for example, that raging when you're angry is likely to

12. Happily Ever After

make you even angrier, and simply smiling when you're sad is likely to make you feel happier.

But when we're emotional, we find it difficult to think straight, and the more strongly we feel, the more likely those feelings will take over our thought process. And this is exactly what I had been experiencing. So only when I took steps to calm my emotions and allow my rational mind to process what I was experiencing, only then did I find happiness.

And after more than 15 years of marriage, I am more happy with love than I ever have been before. We've gone through some schooling, numerous jobs, two pregnancies, and now are facing adolescent daughters. Along the way, we've weathered stress, fights, and depression. But now, more than ever, I love my family, because my family is the most important thing in my life. And I have more confidence now than ever that Margaret and I will be in love through to when the girls graduate, marry, and move out, and beyond. I don't mind jumping in with both feet, even if I don't know where I'll land, as long as Margaret will jump with me.

Since 1983, I've learned some valuable lessons, some of which I wish someone had told me way back when I was a teenager. (Or at least that I wish I had listened to when I was a teenager.)

Some romantic clichés, pulled from romance stories

and movies, are only fanciful expressions of desire, not reality. For example, the cliché is that a woman finds unbridled passion attractive. The reality is that she'll probably find it scary, because she may not understand it, and even if she does, she never knows whether she can control it.

Another one: The cliché is the girl who swoons over a guy who won't return her affections. The reality is that guys do it, too. But when the girls do it, it's endearing and sympathetic. When we do it, it's annoying and maybe even a little creepy.

I always thought I knew less about relationships than my peers, because I always seemed to have more trouble with girls than they did. But now I see that most of my peers also grew up with these feelings and doubts. Now I think, maybe I didn't know less; however, my priorities were different. One of the results is that I have been happily married for over 15 years, never divorced and don't want to be, because that's what I wanted.

And there's a difference between love, sex, and romance. These three are commonly confused in pop culture, but it is possible to feel romantic longing, for example, without thinking about sex. That is, in fact, what I did for a good part of my life. Sex is sex, but romance is attention and affection and tenderness, kissing your partner's cheek and running your fingers

12. Happily Ever After

through her hair and cuddling up to her and caressing her face.

Not everything is about sex, and sex is not just about coitus and climax. A soft kiss, a touch on the breast, it gives attention and shows affection, but it doesn't always have to lead to sex. But in a healthy relationship, sex, romance, and love are all interrelated. Sex provides romance, touching, intimacy, communication, and it's also an act of love. Acts of love are romantic, and the romance makes one want to love his partner more.

It is said that romance happens at the beginning of a relationship, and then it fades. But this too is not entirely correct. Romantic feelings come and go, as do all feelings, circumstantial, untargeted, chemical memories washing through the mind and body. And when they come, simply direct them toward your lover, because she deserves it.

Similarly, the sex isn't necessarily best at the beginning of a relationship, because there are always new things to try. If you doubt this, just spend a little time studying sexual technique on the Internet. For example, did you know that several important erogenous zones are located on the back—I've counted a dozen potential erogenous zones on the body, and that's before you even get to the good parts. Even in a mature relationship, there are new ways to touch, new experiences to explore. And it's always fun when you can explore them together.

The most important sexual skill one can learn is communication, because that's how you know what will pleasure your partner and how she will know what pleasures you. Not every person is exactly alike. So what's the best way to please a woman in bed? Talk with her.

This is also what makes sex better and better as a marriage goes on. Only when you're intimate with the same partner over a long period of time can you become *proficient* in being intimate with her. Frankly, my first time was anticlimactic. Years later, however, and the sex is better than ever.

But the most important thing in a relationship is love. And by "love," I don't mean romantic feelings, and I don't mean sexual desire. Love is an unconditional commitment and an action to carry out that commitment. It is not talk; it is not feel; it is *do*. Unconditional love gives you the confidence and stability to face your partner, to expose your insides to her, to become vulnerable to her, without fear that she'll hate you or leave you for who you are. I could not have written or published this story, with all of its dwelling on old girls and old romances, unless Margaret and I unconditionally loved and trusted each other. But because we do, finishing the story has left me more in love with her

12. Happily Ever After

than when I started.

See, true love isn't about passion or lust or attraction or common interests and personalities or any of the other things they tell you that you need in a relationship. Love is something altogether different. It's about learning to complement each other, learning to grow with each other. It's about doing love-things, even when you don't feel like it, even when life drives you to the edge of insanity, even if you think you've lost love. It's about commitment and perseverance and thinking and feeling and happiness. And I thank God every day that I've found it.

Romantic Poems

Following is a selection of romantic poetry I have written through the years. All of these poems were written to specific girls. Most of them were never delivered. Likewise, not all are suitable for wooing. Rather, they simply reflect the passion that was within me, whether of happiness or of angst.

Lifelong Romance

Let me hold you in my arms
And kiss your sweet lips.
Let me pet your lovely hair
And caress your beautiful face.

Let me look deep into your eyes,
And you into mine.
Come stand by me,
And we will be together always.

Our relationship has bloomed,
Like a flower,
From a desolate nothingness
Into an indescribable love.

Come wrap your arms around me;
Kiss me, and I will do the same.
We can love each other forever
Until we die.

To the One I Love

How should I show
The one I love
How I love her?

If I knew how
To make it known,
That would I do.

But the fact is
I fear that she
Would not understand.

Do you know
The things I see
Hidden in you?

I see the hurt
You have from those
For whom you care.

I see the joy
Of new-made hearts
That you can express.

All that you think
I understand
And will support.

All that you feel
I would feel too
If I were there.

All that you are
is what I love
Because it is you.

If it has seemed
As though it were
Not as I say,

I ask you
To understand
My love is this:

The things you do
And what you think
Are yours to work through.

And if you ever need me,
I will be right here for you.

Thinking of You

Thoughts of you
>Make me cry.
>>I pour my heart to no one.

Affections

The thought occurred to me before the time
I told you of the whisper I had heard,
And so I've written you this little rhyme
In order that your feelings might be stirred.
Your manner, strong reality portrayed,
Yet sweetened rightly by your strong embrace,
Makes smooth the path in which my life is stayed,
And finds my heart of sleep without a trace.
Your eyes are sapphires shining brightly blue;
They glow like planets seen on cloudless nights.
Your hair is scented with the morning dew;
Its lovely long, dark strands caress my sights.
But what is one to do with love like this,
Unwanted, unaccepted, and amiss?

If Only I Could Have Your Love

If only my heart could fly like a bird,
Or my soul like a plane.
If only one word could be uttered
To express the affection inside.

And if only that because we were friends
I could be your lover,
For the sake of the love that has grown
And will grow if it is allowed.

If only my inadequacies could be redefined,
So that the rejection I feel
Would be turned instead to motivation,
Driving me ever forward, closer to you.

When the last of my friends has forsaken me
I'd like to think that you'd still be there,
Because, even though I used to think that
    it could never work,
I strongly and sincerely hoped that I could be wrong.

If only the world were really "only this big,"
So that there would indeed be room for the both of us.

Blue and Grey

Lonely eyes, blue and grey,
In them I can see my frightened child run away.
Seeking love in a maze of unopened doors,
She has no idea that I have what she's looking for.

And darkness covers all the lies.
It rips through her disguise.
I wonder, will she ever come home again.

Look at me; I'm waiting for you.
I was here while life abused and abandoned you.
Blow after blow, time after time,
But they beat me, too, and no one seemed to mind.

And loves, they leave you every time,
And the loves that don't, they die.
But I will never ever leave you, my friend.

I love you more than you'll ever know.

Oh, my frightened child,
Look to me; I have the answer.

And loves, they left you every time,

But my love will never die.

No, I'll never ever ever leave you, my friend.

Dear Tracy...

Inasmuch as the world could have stopped turning
    about its axis,
Spinning around and around as it has
    for centuries past and will continue
    for centuries to come,
Could I, in such a short time, stop loving you.

For, as I have attempted to display,
I have immensely enjoyed the times
    we've spent together,
Holding hands, talking, kissing, hugging, touching...

You do not realize the impact you have had on my life,
In this so short a time, for I know

That you do not value yourself highly enough
    to have had this effect,
Although I value you more highly than this,

That you do not feel the closeness
    and desire for greater closeness
    which comes from the closeness
    we have both displayed for each other,
As I do.

That you are helplessly and hopelessly addicted
    to abuse and abandonment;
Even though I have tried my level best
    To be a true lover,
    To describe to you the incredible commitment
        I have in store for one woman,
    To treat you as an equal, not a subservient,
    As a woman, not an object,
    As an independent person capable of thought,
        rather than a mindless animal
        whose instincts are its sole guide,
    As a human being, who is entitled to doubts,
        fears, strong emotions,
        beautiful passions...
    Regarding you as important
        as anyone I've ever known;

However, you choose not to accept me as such;
You choose to instead take the love of a man who,
    I am sure,
Will not know you, respect you, or love you.

Margaret

I am so glad that you feel comfortable with me,
    Margaret.
In this, my soul takes joy!
For I have longed for one with whom I can express
    the deepest desires of my heart
Without rejection.

I love you!

I am so enthralled with your beauty, Margaret,
Not only of the flesh, but also of the heart.
For I have waited for one who will share with me
    a part of herself.

I love you!

I am so content to commit myself to you, Margaret,
Both for the moment and for the rest of my life.
For the most important thing in my life now is
    my love for you,
And you are the most important person.

And although these few words do not begin to express
>the deepness of my love for you,
I know that it will grow further and deeper,
Ever broadening into each of our lives,
Even our personalities,
Until each of us knows that he can unconditionally
>not survive without the other.

I love you!

Pine

The following is a short, fictional coming-of-age story. See if you can notice my own experiences reflected in Jace's.

Each morning Jace walked by her house on his way to school. Each afternoon he passed it on his way home. Sometimes, he also passed at other times. Occasionally he caught a glimpse of the bright-faced girl with wavy blonde locks. She sat under the two conifers that towered overhead. But as far as he knew, she never noticed him.

The house itself, a grey Stick Victorian with brown trim, spoke of a happy family. Its expansive porch took a jaunt through the sweet-scented yellows and reds of the flower garden. Little gabled alcoves jutted into the world, embraced by the overall form of the structure, as if its gables were parents looking after their offspring. A squat wall of white stone stood, isolating the yard from the public sidewalk, making up in intensity what it lacked in stature, a formidable protector to all within.

But the trees were even more special, for under these Jennifer would read. Or sometimes she would just be sitting quietly or humming softly a tune Jace didn't recognize. Jace paid her no heed, or else she might see his admiration. But out of the corner of his eye, he noticed her shapely form, and he fought to keep breathing. And in his imagination, he felt the softness of her pink cashmere sweater in his delicate hands. He felt her fingers running through his thick, dark hair. Her chocolate eyes and his ordinary brown ones got lost in each other. Perhaps his finger stroked the line of her eyebrow, following her face around softly-curved cheek and jaw, finally resting under her chin.

But Jace said nothing, made no motion out of the ordinary. He merely continued walking, as nonchalantly as possible for a big-footed, lanky teen in a grey tee and worn khakis.

Jennifer walked into second-period Algebra wearing a close-fitting, short-sleeved salmon top and jeans. Jace looked up to see her flip her hair over her shoulder, sending a scented breeze wafting over his face.

In fifth-period study hall, Jennifer read. Jace took out a pencil and sketchbook, and he drew. From his seat two rows behind hers, Jace filled a page with sketches. At one point, Jennifer peered in his direction. Jace quickly buried himself in the papers on his desk. It was only partially an act. From his mental snapshot, he saw dark eyes, sultry, staring at him, which with talent and skill he transferred to the page.

In sixth-period English class, Jennifer sat at the desk directly in front of Jace. At one point, she turned to him. "I broke my pencil. Do you have an extra I could borrow?"

"Yeah." He always carried surplus sharp pencils. Jace handed one to her.

The bell rang signaling the end of the day. As Jace started his walk home, Jennifer caught up to him.

"Jace!" She proffered the borrowed pencil. "Here's your pencil. Thanks."

He took it, but just for a moment, she held on to the pencil, would not release her grip, and Jace wondered whether she wanted to keep it. As far as he was concerned, she could. It was only a pencil.

"You were really a life-saver," she said.

"It was no big deal," Jace replied. It was only a pencil; he had only saved her a trip to the pencil sharpener.

"Well, thanks anyway."

They talked as they walked, mostly trivia—school, the weather, the ball game—until they reached Jennifer's house.

"Well, this is me," she said.

Jace said nothing.

"Can I show you something?"

Jennifer led him up the path and under the tall

trees.

"This is one of my favorite spots," she said.

The shade was cool, and the air smelled of pine. Birds sung through a light breeze, which gently vibrated the branches in an awkward motion Jace could never figure out. Jennifer leaned against one of the trees.

"Sometimes I imagine standing under these trees and getting kissed by a boy I really like." She giggled coyly. "It's just a silly fantasy."

She rubbed her foot through the blanket of needles underneath. Then her gaze met his.

"I guess everyone has silly fantasies like that sometimes."

"Yeah, I guess so."

"I'd love to see some of your drawings," she said.

"Huh?"

"I saw you drawing a picture one time. It was pretty good. It looked like you did it a lot."

Jace was mortified. "Um, yeah, I guess I do."

"Sorry," she said. "You don't have to if you don't want."

He pulled from his book bag a sketchpad. "Here," he said, and handed it to her.

They sat next to each other under the trees, and she opened the first page to reveal a rough rendering of a house. On the next page some neighborhood kids played at the playground down the street. Then came a local road with cars, a bicycle and rider, someone working in an office.

She turned the page again, and her own face gazed back at her as if she were looking into a mirror. But the face in the mirror was beautiful, suave, womanly, yet still young. It was the face of a supermodel, but not fake like supermodels can be; it was a real person, of flesh and blood and graphite.

"Oh my."

Jace tensed and his heart beat faster.

Jennifer swallowed. "This is really good."

"Thanks."

The page after that was a collage of Jennifer. She was cute, sophisticated, sexy, humble, studious, and numerous other qualities for which there are no words.

Jace panicked. "Sorry." He fumbled with words. "I didn't, uh, mean to, um, stalk you— or anything."

Jennifer didn't look angry or scared as she looked him in the eye. She took a breath. "Will you kiss me?"

Having previously only fantasized of the moment, Jace was now confused by the reality of it. Not knowing what to do, he froze, eyes wide and transfixed, unable to move forward, unable to run away. He could almost reach out with his mind and bridge the gap. But not all of the will power in the world would alone solidify these vibrant images and give them physical form.

Dizzy, as if in a dream, he touched his lips to hers, soft and full. She smelled good. He put his arm around her, and his hand passed over the strap of her bra. Her body was warm and there. She put her hand on his leg.

A moment later, he counted her eyelashes. He touched his thumb to her eyebrow and traced it around, and Jennifer snuggled her cheek into Jace's palm. Her skin was soft. It was smooth. And she looked happy.

"I like you, Jace," she managed. Then, with a lost smile, "I wish I wasn't moving."

"You're moving?"

"Yes, to Seattle."

"That's pretty far," he said.

"Yes, it is."

"It sure is."

"Can you sit with me for a little while?"

The next day, Jace had to walk on the grass as he passed by the house, because the green and white moving van was taking up the whole sidewalk. He hoped to catch a glimpse of Jennifer, but she was nowhere to be seen.

Now when Jace walks by the house, he sometimes sees two young children playing in the yard. Jace has

Jennifer's new address, and they've exchanged one or two letters. But he doesn't know whether he'll ever see her again. He figures, even if you're an artist, sometimes you draw dead. Still he imagines he sees Jennifer sitting under the pines, reading or humming softly a tune he doesn't know.

Read more anecdotes of the author's past, present, and future. Point your web browser at *J. Timothy King's Blog*:

```
http://blog.JTimothyKing.com/
```

Also keep up to date with new book releases and special offers, limited book bundles, and gift discounts.

www.ingramcontent.com/pod-product-compliance
Lightning Source LLC
LaVergne TN
LVHW011424080426
835512LV00005B/259